Kristal.hoy83@gmail.com

P9-DFZ-450

THE JESUS-CENTERED LIFE

The life you didn't think was possible,
with the Jesus you never knew

RICK LAWRENCE

The Jesus-Centered Life

Copyright © 2016 Rick Lawrence / 0000 0000 3376 9992

All rights reserved. No part of this book may be reproduced in any manner whatsoever without prior written permission from the publisher, except where noted in the text and in the case of brief quotations embodied in critical articles and reviews. For information, email inforights@group.com, or go to group.com/permissions.

group.com

Credits
Author: Rick Lawrence
Executive Developer: Tim Gilmour
Chief Creative Officer: Joani Schultz
Editors: Rob Cunningham and Rick Edwards
Assistant Editor: Ann Diaz
Art Director: Darrin Stoll
Production Artist: Amber Gomez Balanzar
Cover Art: Jeff Storm
Production Manager: Melissa Towers

Unless otherwise indicated, Scripture quotations are taken from the New American Standard Bible®. Copyright © 1960, 1962, 1963, 1968, 1971, 1972, 1973, 1975, 1977, 1995 by The Lockman Foundation. Used by permission. All rights reserved.

Scripture quotations marked NIV are taken from the Holy Bible, NEW INTERNATIONAL VERSION®, NIV® Copyright © 1973, 1978, 1984, 2011 by Biblica, Inc.® Used by permission. All rights reserved worldwide.

Scripture quotations marked NLT are taken from the *Holy Bible*, New Living Translation, copyright ©1996, 2004, 2007, 2013 by Tyndale House Foundation. Used by permission of Tyndale House Publishers, Inc., Carol Stream, Illinois 60188. All rights reserved.

Scripture quotations marked The Message are taken from The Message. Copyright © 1993, 1994, 1995, 1996, 2000, 2001, 2002. Used by permission of NavPress Publishing Group.

"You Will Go Free" lyrics by Tonio K. from the *Romeo Unchained* album (Gadfly Records, 1996) reprinted with permission.

Any website addresses included in this book are offered only as a resource and/or reference for the reader. The inclusion of these websites is not intended, in any way, to be interpreted as an endorsement of these sites or their content on the part of Group Publishing or the author. In addition, the author and Group Publishing do not vouch for the content of these websites for the life of this book.

ISBN 978-1-4707-2827-4

10 9 8 7 6 5 4 3   23 22 21 20 19 18 17 16

Library of Congress Cataloging-in-Publication Data

Names: Lawrence, Rick, 1961- author.
Title: The Jesus-centered life : the life you didn't think was possible, with the Jesus you never knew / Rick Lawrence.
Description: First American paperback [edition]. | Loveland, Colorado : Group Pub., Inc., 2016. | Includes bibliographical references. | Description based on print version record and CIP data provided by publisher; resource not viewed.
Identifiers: LCCN 2015045623 (print) | LCCN 2015044874 (ebook) | ISBN 9781470728281 (ePub) | ISBN 9781470728274 (pbk.)
Subjects: LCSH: Christian life.
Classification: LCC BV4501.3 (print) | LCC BV4501.3 .L3938 2016 (ebook) | DDC 248.4--dc23
LC record available at http://lccn.loc.gov/2015045623

Table of Contents

—*Part One*—
The Stockdale Way

—Part Two—
The Beeline Practices

A Closing Imperative

Dedication

To the thousands of ministry people who've experienced my eight-hour "Jesus-Centered Ministry" training, and who've urged me for years to write something that's focused on all of life, not just ministry settings.

Acknowledgments

In this season of my life, I'm indebted to so many who have fueled both my passion for Jesus and the completion of this work. I'm first grateful for Andy Brazelton, who was determined to make "Jesus-centered" our defining mission as we engaged ministry people with resources and events, and who offers me inexplicable belief every day. For Thom and Joani Schultz, who not only went to the mat in support of this book but also have been evangelists for its message for a long time. For Tim Gilmour, my longtime boss, for looking out for the readers of this book by highlighting words in the manuscript that perplexed him. For Carl Medearis, who has been a kindred spirit and a prophetic presence in my life at just the right time. For Tom Melton, who continues to be the most catalytic person in my life, apart from my wife. For Bev, who knows me better and loves me more deeply than anyone in my life. For my beloved girls, Lucy and Emma, for making me an insufferable homebody. For Jeff Storm, who designed the J. logo, which was first used on *Jesus-Centered Youth Ministry* and then the *Jesus-Centered Bible*—brilliant. For Rob Cunningham, whose last official responsibility was to edit this manuscript before he left for the choppy waters of a freelance life. For my community of co-workers at Group Publishing, who have fueled my own growth in too many ways to count. For the community represented by the Simply Jesus Gathering, who have generously offered their own personal "beeline practices" throughout this book.

Introduction

Human beings are pretty good at lots of things. There's that whole invention-of-the-light-bulb thing, and sometimes people bowl a strike in every frame, and a few of us know how to throw people in the air and catch them again while we're ice skating. But, universally, maybe the best thing we do as humans is worship. We're hard-wired for it. In fact, we can't stop ourselves from worshipping the people and things that surround us, because worship is as autonomic as breathing. All of us worship a god of some kind—it's just a question of whether the "g" is uppercase or lowercase. Celebrated writer David Foster Wallace says it well: "In the day-to-day trenches of adult life, there is actually no such thing as atheism. There is no such thing as not worshipping. Everybody worships. The only choice we get is *what* to worship."[1]

Some of us worship God-alone, and some of us worship something else (the something-elses are bottomless possibilities). And a *whole lot of us* live in the vast middle of this bell curve—we worship "God-plus." I mean, we mostly say we believe in or think highly of the big-G God, but we like to add a little something-something to our God-worship, such as...

- God-plus-the-American-Dream or...
- God-plus-social-media or...
- God-plus-family-values or...
- God-plus-high-achievement or...
- God-plus-hip-hop-culture or...
- God-plus-sexual-fulfillment or...
- God-plus-the-NFL/NASCAR/Golf-Channel or...
- God-plus self-improvement or...
- God-plus-Starbucks or...
- God-plus-year-round-sports-leagues or...
- God-plus-shopping...

You get the idea. The overwhelming majority of us are God-plus people, because God-only people often seem *extreme*. I mean, they can come off creepy and intense and something-other-than-normal. So we like our God-worship diluted with other kinds of worship, just to take the creepy edge off of it. Another way to describe the God-plus life is the compartmentalized life—we generally like God to stay where he belongs, in the spiritual/religious compartment we've built just for him. It would be rude and awkward for him to wander away from his compartment and camp out on the couch in, for example, our girls/guys-night-out compartment. We love all our compartments and want those walls to stay up. So, broadly speaking, we feel more comfortable telling people we *believe in God* than telling them we *follow Jesus*. And we certainly wouldn't feel relaxed describing our relationship with Jesus using extreme language: People who say things like *I'm ruined for Jesus*, for example, tend to make people back up a step. That kind of description seems awkward, vaguely negative, and (certainly) overly intense. So it's out of the question for all of us, except for the creepy ones...

Now my soul has what you might call an open floor plan. Jesus has permission to walk around in my de-compartmentalized life, messing with my stuff and showing up at all hours of the day, in all situations.

But about a decade ago I had a tipping-point experience that signaled a deep shift in me—it profoundly changed the way I describe myself and redirected my purpose in life. I was like a passenger on a train, crossing a country's border at night while I slept. When I awoke, I discovered that I'd traveled a great distance from the God-plus territory I'd always known and entered into the Jesus-only, *ruined-for-him* landscape where I now live. The country around me was littered with debris—a hurricane named Yeshua had leveled my compartment walls. Now my soul has what you might call an open floor plan. Jesus has permission to walk around in my de-compartmentalized life, messing with my stuff and showing up at all hours of the day, in all situations. And because this de-compartmentalization feels deeply congruent with who I really am, I rarely come off creepy. I'm sticking with that self-assessment.

Here's what happened to me...

The Beauty of Boredom

I'm a Christian ministry leader and a writer and editor and speaker, so I get invited to lead workshops and deliver keynotes at conferences. Ten years ago I was asked by the organizers of a large ministry conference in the Midwest to lead a two-hour session for leaders—they wanted me to do something a little experimental with this group. At the time, I was toying with a way of engaging people that focused every aspect of life and ministry on a deepening relational attachment to Jesus. It was an attempt to explore what life would look like if it was "Jesus-only" instead of "Jesus-plus." I started calling this way of living life and impacting others "Jesus-centered." I'd been speaking around the country for years, drawing from a broad menu of what I'd call the "tips-and-techniques" of ministry. But slowly, subtly, I'd lost my enthusiasm for all of that stuff—people liked hearing something practical that they could write down in their notes, but I realized that my own freedom from captivity had nothing to do with tips-and-techniques. I had experienced transformation through a deepening relationship with and dependence on the person of Jesus, not by trying harder to be a better Christian.

> I had experienced transformation through a deepening relationship with and dependence on the person of Jesus, not by trying harder to be a better Christian.

So as I led this small group of ministry leaders through my half-conceived, seat-of-the-pants spiritual adventure, the room crackled with electricity. We all thought we were merely learning how to morph conventional ways of studying the Bible and praying and serving others into practices that more intentionally focused on Jesus. But what happened, in fact, was that a roomful of people unconsciously moved into a closer orbit around the most magnetic person in the universe.

By the end of those two hours, that little band of 30 or so leaders had barreled into a runaway worship-train. We were crying and laughing and hungry for more of Jesus. And some people in the room, with many years of Christian ministry on their résumés, waited in a long line after the session to tell me a startling revelation: They'd never really tasted this deeply of Jesus before, and had never appreciated his height and depth and breadth. I understood exactly what they were trying to say.

When I emerged from this catalyzing experience, my appetite for knowing Jesus more deeply was voracious. And with my leadership responsibilities completed, I was free to roam the rest of the conference, popping into as many workshops and general sessions as I could cram in. I listened to many of the best ministry experts in the country that day—all of them brilliant, and many of them longtime friends. But by the end of the day, I felt a growing restlessness, even an anxiety. My experience in and out of workshops all day, listening to succeeding lists of spiritual imperatives—the perfectly reasonable tips-and-techniques of the conventional Christian life—had *deadened* my soul.

As evening crept up on me, that deadness spread into a kind of depression. I wandered around the vast, crowded atrium of the conference center in a daze, finally sinking into an overstuffed chair that sat like an island in the middle of a rushing river of people. I needed to pray, to retreat into myself, and it wasn't hard to get lost in the throng. In my little cone of silence, I pleaded with Jesus: "Why, why, why am I feeling this way?" Tears streamed down my cheeks, and my face contorted with pain. I sat quietly weeping, gripped by an inexplicable despair. And then, in one of those moments when the voice of Jesus is clear enough that it's nearly audible, these words cut through my fog:

"You're bored by everything but me now."

Startled, I knew Jesus was telling me the truth as soon as I heard it—his words had the same impact that a sunburst has after a rainy day. My eyes brightened and the weight I felt on my shoulders was suddenly gone. Jesus had explained the mystery of my sadness perfectly, releasing me from my dulling captivity. The "try harder to get better" strategies for spiritual growth I'd been working at my whole adult life now seemed like annoying background noise. As I'd been tasting the intoxicating presence of Jesus more deeply, my conventional God-plus habits seemed worse than bland in comparison. If you showed up at a cooking class that promised a mystery celebrity chef and then discovered Oprah was teaching it, you'd probably be less impressed with her recipes and more interested in *her*.

I'd always defined discipleship as a progression that looked a lot like doing well in school—studying hard, growing in knowledge, doing well on tests. But those things, I realized, now paled in comparison to the undeniable truth: True disciples, people who follow Jesus and live out his mission, are captured and carried away by him. They are so stuck on him that the natural outcome of their attachment to him is a perpetual willingness to give over their lives to him. They can't help themselves anymore—their path of retreat away from Jesus now seems blocked by their driving fascination with him, and their undeniable passion for him. The old building they once called *home*—constructed by the do's and don'ts of the normal Christian life—has been demolished by a wrecking ball forged in Nazareth. And now...*They are ruined by Jesus and ruined for Jesus.*

And they are bored by everything but him...

Everyday Awe

In his excellent book *Jesus Mean and Wild,* author Mark Galli describes what happened when a group of Laotian refugees asked if they could become members of the church he was pastoring. Since these Laotians had little knowledge of Jesus or the Bible, Galli offered to lead them through a study of Mark's Gospel. When Galli got to the passage in Mark 4 where Jesus calms the storm, he asked the refugees to talk about the "storms" in their lives—their problems, worries, and struggles. The people looked confused and puzzled. Finally, one of the Laotian men asked, "Do you mean that Jesus actually calmed the wind and sea in the middle of a storm?" Galli thought the man was struggling to accept this over-the-top story, so he said: "Yes, but we should not get hung up on the details of the miracle. We should remember that Jesus can calm the storms in our lives." After another uncomfortable silence, another man spoke up: "Well, if Jesus calmed the wind and the waves, he must be a very powerful man!" The Laotians buzzed with excitement and worship. And while these newbie Christian refugees were having a transcendent experience with a Jesus they'd only just met, Galli realized he'd so taken Jesus for granted that he'd missed him altogether.[2]

As I've been living my new reality for more than a decade now, I've accidentally discovered this truth: When the living, breathing Jesus is the center of everything in our lives, fruit happens. That's just the way things work. Good things grow in our soul, and we can give to others out of our abundance. We don't have to spend all our energy trying to produce that fruit anymore than a shriveled, neglected tree—dying from thirst—has to work to produce fruit once its roots have been watered and fertilized. Jesus promised "living water" for a reason—he knows we are created by God to live fruitful lives, but we can't grow a thing if we don't know how to abide in him. Abiding in him means drinking deeply from his well of living water, and that water is like Miracle-Gro® for the soul.

I've accidentally discovered this truth: When the living, breathing Jesus is the center of everything in our lives, fruit happens.

"Apart from me, you can do nothing," Jesus says, delivering a blunt diagnosis and an unbelievable invitation in the same breath. *The implication is that when we abide in him, we can do anything.*

We are meant to live in everyday awe with Jesus. As he becomes the consuming focus of our worship, we discover the last number on our life's combination lock, and we taste true freedom and purpose for the first time. Jesus' life and energy flows through us, transforming our life into a "moveable feast" that nourishes the hungry people who enter our orbit. I met David, a vibrant 70-year-old man with eager eyes, at a friend's party, and discovered he'd lived an incredible life. In his spare time, for example, he'd climbed Denali, the tallest mountain in North America, and all 53 of Colorado's "14ers." When I learned he'd been a passionate follower of Jesus all his life, I asked what the key to his "long obedience in the same direction" was. And he didn't miss a beat: "It's all about worship." I waited for more...but he said no more.

We are meant to live in everyday awe with Jesus. As he becomes the consuming focus of our worship, we discover the last number on our life's combination lock, and we taste true freedom and purpose for the first time.

Do you long to find the well of living water David drinks from?

Do you hear a quiet voice inside you asking: "Is this all there is?"

Has the "normal Christian life" left you discontent and bored?

Do you gravitate toward God-plus pursuits because he often doesn't seem big enough to handle all the problems and challenges you face in life? Or, simply, he's not as compelling as all those other pluses?

Well, what if you discovered that a life of everyday awe is possible and sustainable for everyday people who will never climb Denali? What if the small, manageable, comfortable, and dulling God you've been disciplining yourself to follow is actually bigger, more beautiful, and more thrilling than the normal Christian life has led you to believe? What if Jesus seems so familiar to you that you've stopped experiencing him as he really is? It doesn't matter, really, what your current reality is. The only thing that matters is your curiosity—the desire to walk a little further into the "deep magic," as the *Chronicles of Narnia* author C.S. Lewis calls it.[3]

You're already worshipping something(s) in your life—that's a given. And one of those somethings is probably some version of God, along with your own stockpile of pluses. What if, instead, you gathered all your worship-chips into one big pile and shoved them into the middle of the table, to the spot marked "Jesus"? What if you decided to go all-in with him—to take the biggest risk of your life on the safest bet in the universe? Well, I don't think you should do that just because I think it's a good idea, or because the church says you should. No, I think you'll end up shoving all your chips onto that Jesus-spot when you discover, maybe for the first time, that you can't help yourself.

Endnotes

1 David Foster Wallace, *This Is Water: Some Thoughts, Delivered on a Significant Occasion, About Living a Compassionate Life* (New York, NY: Little, Brown and Company, 2009), 96-101.

2 Mark Galli, *Jesus Mean and Wild: The Unexpected Love of an Untamable God* (Grand Rapids, MI: Baker Books, 2006), 112.

3 C.S. Lewis, *The Lion, the Witch, and the Wardrobe* (New York, NY: HarperCollins, 2008), 83.

—Part One—
The Stockdale Way

Vice Admiral Jim Stockdale was one of the most highly decorated officers in U.S. Navy history. At the outset of the Vietnam War, he piloted an F-8 Crusader during the aerial attack of three North Vietnamese torpedo boats in what was later called the Gulf of Tonkin Incident. Later, in 1965, his fighter was hit by enemy fire and he was forced to eject. He parachuted into an enemy village, where he was captured and severely beaten. Dragging a shattered leg from the beating, he was taken to the infamous "Hanoi Hilton," where he was imprisoned for nearly eight years—the highest-ranking prisoner of war in the U.S. Navy. While there, he led a prisoner resistance movement and created a secret code of conduct that all prisoners pledged to uphold, including the proper response to torture. Because of his rank and his involvement in the resistance, he was relentlessly and ruthlessly tortured. Eventually, he and nearly a dozen other prisoners were taken to a nearby holding facility dubbed "Alcatraz," where Stockdale lived in a 3-foot-by-9-foot cell with a light bulb that burned around the clock. He and the other prisoners at Alcatraz were locked in leg irons every night.

Remarkably, Stockdale survived this horrific experience. He was released in February 1973—his body so broken that he could barely walk. After he'd recovered from his injuries enough to live a more active life, he finished his naval career as president of the Naval War College. He went on to a distinguished career in public service and politics: He was Ross Perot's 1992 vice presidential running mate when Perot won 19 percent of the popular vote—the best showing by an independent ticket in modern U.S. electoral history. When bestselling author Jim Collins was later introduced to Stockdale at a social gathering, he was quickly mesmerized by the war hero's story. Collins asked Stockdale how he managed to not only make it out of the Hanoi Hilton with an unbroken spirit, but how he'd been able to live a productive, vigorous life after he was released. Stockdale responded: "I never lost faith in the end of the story, I never doubted not only that I would get out, but also that I would prevail in the end and turn the experience into the defining event of my life, which, in retrospect, I would not trade."[1]

Stockdale's response was so profound that Collins made it the center of one of the most popular business-leadership books of all time: *Good to Great*. Collins translated the vice admiral's key to surviving and thriving in the midst of unendurable circumstances into something he dubbed the "Stockdale Paradox":

"You must never confuse faith that you will prevail in the end—which you can never afford to lose—with the discipline to confront the most brutal facts of your current reality, whatever they might be."[2]

As a P.S. to this paradox, Collins later asked Stockdale about those who didn't make it out of the Hanoi Hilton alive, as he had. Collins wanted to know what was different about those who didn't survive. "Oh, that's easy," replied Stockdale, "[they were] optimists. Oh, they were the ones who said, 'We're going to be out by Christmas.' And Christmas would come, and Christmas would go. Then they'd say, 'We're going to be out by Easter.' And Easter would come, and Easter would go. And then Thanksgiving, and then it would be Christmas again. And they died of a broken heart."[3]

Optimism offers false hope because it is not married to brutal reality. *To experience true freedom, it's necessary for us to embrace both our brutal realities and our prevailing hope at the same time.* Jesus, it turns out, operates all of the time in the tension of the Stockdale Paradox. He is always and everywhere exposing brutal realities while pressing forward into prevailing hopes. He blows the lid off the scandalous and humiliating secret life of the woman at the well and then offers her the living water her soul is desperately thirsty for (John 4:7-29). He responds to the Canaanite woman, desperate for Jesus to release her daughter from demonic bondage, by calling her a "dog" and refusing to help, but then quickly gives her what she wants when she rises to his challenge (Matthew 15:21-28). After his resurrection, he asks his closest friend Peter three times if he really loves him; he follows each painful question with a life-giving invitation: "Feed my sheep" (John 21:15-18, NLT).

Following Jesus wholeheartedly means facing the "most brutal facts of our current reality, whatever they might be" while holding onto our absolute certainty that we will "prevail in the end" through his love and grace. Many are familiar with the preamble to theologian Reinhold Niebuhr's famous "Serenity Prayer," but few know well the payload portion of the prayer that follows. Here's how it begins…

God grant me the serenity
to accept the things I cannot change;
courage to change the things I can;
and wisdom to know the difference.

A pithy quote that reads well taped to the refrigerator door, no doubt. But Niebuhr, one of the great intellectuals in Christian history, is no lightweight. He's exploring deeper territory—Stockdale Paradox territory—in the conclusion of his prayer…

Living one day at a time;
enjoying one moment at a time;
accepting hardships as the pathway to peace;
taking, as He did, this sinful world
as it is, not as I would have it;
trusting that He will make all things right
if I surrender to His Will;
that I may be reasonably happy in this life
and supremely happy with Him
forever in the next.
Amen.[4]

Do you sense the tension in Niebuhr's confluence of brutal reality and prevailing hope? True serenity, we learn, lives in the liminal space of this tension. We cup our hands to hold both truths—the truth of how things really are, and the truth of how things really will be—and drink deeply. This is the living water Jesus offers us.

And so, in the first section of this book, we'll lean into some brutal realities while simultaneously embracing some prevailing hopes that will fuel our journey.

And so, in the first section of this book, we'll lean into some brutal realities while simultaneously embracing some prevailing hopes that will fuel our journey.

In the second section, we'll explore the everyday rhythms and simple practices that will draw us into a deeper relationship with Jesus, who is the embodiment of our prevailing hope. We'll discover that the Stockdale Paradox is so much more than a survival technique or a foundation for great leadership—it's God's circadian rhythm.

Endnotes

1 Quoted from a keynote address by Jim Collins at the "Drucker Centennial" event on September 1, 2010, in Claremont, California.

2 Jim Collins, *Good to Great: Why Some Companies Make the Leap...and Others Don't* (New York: HarperCollins, 2010), 13.

3 Ibid, 83-85.

4 From the "Queries and Answers" column in *The New York Times Book Review* (July 2, 1950), 23.

1

Embracing Our Brutal Realities

"I have loved you even as the Father has loved me. Remain in my love."

—Jesus

Jesus is the most-known, least-known person in human history.

There has never been a more widely recognizable name on earth. But, in turn, there has never been a more widely misunderstood, misquoted, mischaracterized, miseverything-ed person than the homeless rabbi from Nazareth.

Every year since 1927 *Time Magazine* has named a "Person of the Year" on its January cover. In 2013 *Time*'s editors decided to one-up themselves and name the most significant person in history. So, after an exhaustive analysis that ranked historical figures just as Google ranks Web pages, Jesus won out—it wasn't even close.

Of course, Jesus is the single most influential person in history—it doesn't matter whether you worship him as God or mark your birthday by the year of his death or repeat something he said without even realizing he said it ("Do to others whatever you would like them to do to you" or "He sends rain on the just and the unjust" or "Tomorrow will bring its own worries," for example). His words and his deeds have done more to shape our world, and our everyday lives, than any other single force.

So it's a little ironic that just before *Time* put Jesus on its "Most Significant Person in History" cover, editors at *Newsweek* recruited the University of North Carolina's resident Jesus-skeptic Bart Ehrman to write an article titled "What Do We Really Know About Jesus?" In it, the religious studies professor skewers a handful of contradictory details surrounding Jesus' birth and soft-peddles the historical reality of Jesus with this summation of the Gospel accounts of his life, death, and resurrection: "These are books that meant to declare religious truths, not historical facts."[1]

Sure, we know Jesus. But the way we're still wrangling over the details of his existence exposes a blunt reality: We don't *know* Jesus. And I wish I was merely describing a dynamic that exists outside the church, the place where we often *assume* everybody knows and believes in Jesus. But those who identify themselves as Christians seem just as confused. Well over a third of churched people (39 percent) believe there's a good possibility that Jesus sinned when he walked the earth. More than half (58 percent) say the Holy Spirit, who's identified in Scripture as "the Spirit of Jesus" (Acts 16:7; Philippians 1:19) is merely a symbol, not a living entity.[2] A Jesus who sins, and a Jesus who concocts elaborate lies about the Spirit, is a scam artist, not the Son of God, worthy of worship. Posers and fakers and liars do not meet the stringent job requirements for "God."

In one way or another, a lot of us believe in a Jesus who's not Jesus at all.

No More Mr. Nice Guy

I was talking with a junior high girl who'd just served as a leader in a church-wide worship experience during Holy Week. She'd spent several days leading people from her congregation into a deeper relationship with Jesus through an interactive devotional experience. The girl was giddy with excitement about the whole thing. I told her I like to ask people to describe Jesus to me—just because I'm curious about how they see him.

"So," I asked, "what are some words you'd use to describe Jesus to someone who's never heard of him?"

She scrunched her forehead and tried to wrestle that question to the ground. Finally, she offered this hopeful response: "Well, I'd have to say he's really, really nice."

She was ready to leave it right there, so I asked: "Remember that time Jesus made a whip and chased all the money changers out of the Temple? Does that story change the way you'd describe Jesus?"

She scrunched her forehead again. The smile disappeared from her face. I'd created a kind of intolerable dissonance in her. Finally, with a tone of desperation, she landed on this: "Well, I know Jesus is nice, so what he did must have been nice." I nodded politely and thanked her for thinking through her response. And then I got an idea. What if I asked people all over the country the same question? Maybe I could find some common threads in their responses. So I recruited videographers in five major metropolitan areas to stop young people randomly on the street and ask them a simple question: "How would you describe Jesus?"

When I got all the raw footage back, I quickly discovered my experience with the junior high girl wasn't an aberration. Without fail, the first and favorite descriptive word Millennials choose for Jesus is always *nice*.[3] And, it turns out, people of *all ages* use similar words to describe him. Search online list-surveys and you'll find these one-word descriptions of Jesus popping up most often: loving, peaceful, forgiving, peacemaker, meek, forgiving, revitalizing, pure, gentle, and humble.[4] "Nice" is a perfect umbrella for these sweet descriptions.

There's nothing wrong with "nice," except it completely misses the ferocious and disruptive impact Jesus had on almost everyone he met.

There's nothing wrong with "nice," except it completely misses the ferocious and disruptive impact Jesus had on almost everyone he met. He's the original bull in a china shop. Is Jesus nice? Yes, of course, but when he is, he's *scandalously nice*. He's nice to all the wrong people, and he's offensive to all the wrong people. Jesus is nice to the people he heals or feeds or rescues. But he'd never be voted Mr. Congeniality. He's definitely un-nice when he's blasting (over and over) religious leaders or calling his lead disciple "Satan" or an innocent Canaanite woman a "dog" or telling the rich young ruler to sell all his possessions and follow him if he intends to inherit eternal life. In Matthew 23 (The Message), Jesus tells the Pharisees they are "hopeless"—not once, but *seven times* in a row—and then he plants three exclamation marks at the end of that diatribe, calling them "manicured grave plots," "total frauds," and "snakes." The good doctor Luke describes Jesus as the social equivalent of a live grenade:

When Jesus had finished speaking, a Pharisee invited him to eat with him; so he went in and reclined at the table. But the Pharisee, noticing that Jesus did not first wash before the meal, was surprised. Then the Lord said to him, "Now then, you Pharisees clean the outside of the cup and dish, but inside you are full of greed and wickedness. You foolish people! Did not the one who made the outside make the inside also? But give what is inside the dish to the poor, and everything will be clean for you. Woe to you Pharisees, because you give God a tenth of your mint, rue and all other kinds of garden herbs, but you neglect justice and the love of God. You should have practiced the latter without leaving the former undone. Woe to you Pharisees, because you love the most important seats in the synagogues and greetings in the marketplaces. Woe to you, because you are like unmarked graves, which men walk over without knowing it." One of the experts in the law answered him, "Teacher, when you say these things, you insult us also" (Luke 11:37-45, NIV).

This awkward, scandalous scene barrels toward disaster after verse 45, with Jesus essentially responding, "Yes, I'm aware I'm insulting you, and I'm just getting started." Wow, someone get Jesus a plate of pasta and a glass of red wine—quick! I'm guessing word spread quickly and the A-listers in the Pharisee's social set scratched Mr. Woe off their dinner-party lists.

Rejecting Lesser Gods

The point here is that a *merely* nice Jesus is *no Jesus at all*—and it's impossible to have an intimate relationship with a person who doesn't really exist, with a *fake* Jesus. In his foreword to *Jesus Mean and Wild,* Eugene Peterson writes: "Every omitted detail of Jesus, so carefully conveyed to us by the Gospel writers, reduces Jesus. We need the whole Jesus. The complete Jesus. Everything he said. Every detail of what he did."[5] And the reason we need the "complete Jesus" is that our false caricatures have relegated him to the wallpaper of our lives. Because we have nice-ified him, he's not all that interesting to us. We habitually diminish Jesus from *shocking* to *average*. Philosophy professor and C.S. Lewis scholar Dr. Peter Kreeft once told his class of Boston University students:

Christ changed every human being he ever met…. If anyone claims to have met him without being changed, he has not met him at all. When you touch him, you touch lightning…. The Greek word used to describe everyone's reaction to him in the Gospels is "thauma"—wonder. This was true of his enemies, who killed him. Of his disciples, who worshipped him. And even of agnostics, who went away shaking their heads and muttering "No man ever spoke like this man" and knowing that if he didn't stop being what he was and saying what he said that eventually they would have to side with either his killers or his worshippers. For "Jesus shock" breaks your heart in two and forces you to choose which half of your heart you will follow….[6]

We habitually diminish Jesus from *shocking* to *average*.

If the Jesus you're trying to know and follow is more like an adult version of Barney, the cuddly children's show dinosaur, than "the lion of the tribe of Judah" or the shocking person that Kreeft is describing, your connection to him will devolve into a compartmentalized, Jesus-plus transaction, not a real relationship with a real person. The false Jesus of our conventional narratives—our Fifty-Shades-of-Nice Jesus—arouses no passion in us. Our latent passivity toward him is a natural result of the milquetoast descriptions we've embraced about him and the tips-and-techniques bastardizations of the things he said and did. It's as if, again, we've become fixated on Oprah's recipes, waxing poetic (and on and on) about them while neglecting to pursue an intimate friendship with the fascinating person who created the recipes in the first place.

And a declawed Jesus doesn't seem strong and fierce and *big* enough to walk with us into the fiery furnaces of everyday life. We're all facing big challenges and struggles, and we're looking for someone or something to help us overcome or give us the courage we need to survive the blows we've endured and the difficult situations we must find our way through. *The Tonight Show*'s Jimmy Fallon is a nice, likeable, relentlessly upbeat guy—he'd be No. 1 on your dream birthday-party list. But you wouldn't choose him as your "wingman" if you were walking into a dark alley in a bad part of town. Nice Jesus isn't hard enough or tough enough or fierce enough to journey with us into our own dark alleys of life—and that's exactly why we need to have a deeper, more real experience of him. If the only Jesus we've experienced in the church is a cardigan-wearing, lullaby-loving Mr. Rogers knockoff, then we'll naturally go all-in with lesser gods that promise better results in the real world.

A declawed Jesus doesn't seem strong and fierce and *big* enough to walk with us into the fiery furnaces of everyday life.

The documentary *The Armstrong Lie* explores the Lance Armstrong doping scandal from an unusual perspective. Instead of rehashing the facts of Armstrong's long and persistent deception—the legendary cyclist who denied using performance-enhancing drugs was later exposed as a serial cheater and stripped of his seven Tour de France victories—the film explores why people for so long refused to accept the bitter truth about him. In the face of overwhelming evidence of his guilt, many refused to believe his accusers and defended him as a hero who'd overcome testicular cancer to power his way to the top of the cycling world. Armstrong was a "lesser god" to many, and it's very hard to give up on those in whom we invest our hope and belief. The film is really about our relentless pursuit of lesser gods and our passionate enmeshment with them. We've always preferred more approachable, more tangible gods to Jesus, and our "Lance

Armstrongs" promise that we can have a more concrete connection with a god who will give us hope while requiring almost nothing of us but our trust and belief.[7]

We don't have to dig too deeply to find evidence that proves this uncomfortable reality. In the aftermath of Nelson Mandela's funeral, for example, a young South African spoken-word artist named Thabiso Mohare wrote a poem in honor of the great anti-apartheid leader. Here's a portion of "An Ordinary Man":

And we watched the world weep
For a giant bigger than myths
A life owned by many
Now free as the gods[8]

"Worshipful" is the best way to describe the tone that infuses this poem, and all the other tributes that framed Mandela's death and funeral. And that makes sense, because Mandela was an amazing man who sacrificed his life, over and over, to win his people their freedom. Our hearts long for heroes to worship. And it's simply easier, and more socially acceptable, to worship lesser gods like Nelson Mandela (or Mother Teresa or Bill Gates or Lady Gaga or Warren Buffett) than it is to worship the rock of offense—the one called "Scandalon"—who is Jesus. We like our lions to be transcendent and bigger-than-life, but also fully human. The "fully God" aspect of Jesus is what unnerves us.

We like our lions to be transcendent and bigger-than-life, but also fully human. The "fully God" aspect of Jesus is what unnerves us.

Our Mid-Marriage Malaise

We have all the evidence we need that our fragile cultural commitment to churchgoing, dragged down by the relentless way we've diminished the real Jesus into an exceptionally well-behaved Middle Eastern philosopher, may not survive the next decade. According to a landmark Pew Research Center survey of 35,000 Americans, the percentage of people who identify as Christian has dropped a whopping 8 percentage points (from 78.4 to 70.6) in just seven years, from 2007 to 2014. This steep dive is over-represented by young adults in the massive Millennial generation (18- to 34-year-olds). Mainline Protestant churches and Catholic churches are also over-represented in the decline. Meanwhile, during the same time frame, the percentage of people who identify as atheist, agnostic, or "nothing in particular" rocketed up by almost 7 points, from 16.1 to 22.8. Pew's associate director of religion research, Greg Smith, who was also the lead researcher on the new study, says: "We've known that the religiously unaffiliated has been growing for decades. But the pace at which they've continued to grow is really astounding."[9]

Yes, the U.S. church is in trouble—more than 200,000 congregations are in decline. Every year, more than 4,000 of them close their doors for good. The people who've managed to stick with the church have a higher average age than the general population; and if you backtrack through the generations you'll find that the younger we are, the less likely we are to be connected with a church. Of course, the U.S. continues to be a religious nation—95 percent of Americans believe in God. But the weekly church attendance figure hovers around 15 percent (the number pegged by researchers who actually count Sunday attenders).[10]

Those who name themselves "Christian" just aren't getting who Jesus really is.

It's clear that despite the best intentions of the Western church—all of our Bible studies, our men's prayer breakfasts, our women's candlelight dinners, our Christian living books, our three-point sermons that load a half-dozen new imperatives onto our backs, our "positive, encouraging" Christian music, and our accountability relationships—those who name themselves "Christian" just aren't getting who Jesus really is. Or we're not getting *enough* of who he really is, or we're getting, literally, a fake Jesus.

And a half-hearted commitment to a Jesus who doesn't really exist won't fuel a lasting connection to the body of Christ. If we were feasting on the real Jesus, as he implored us to do over and over in the sixth chapter of John's Gospel, we'd have the same problems we've always had with the institutional church, but we'd feel compelled by our ruined-for-Jesus love to stick it out together—to live together under the umbrella of our passion for him and to change the things that don't reflect the true goal of the church, which is fueling a growing intimacy with Jesus. "Ruined for" means you stay, even when you'd like to go.

Here's what this dynamic looks like. The Barna Research Group says that 6 out of 10 young-adult Millennials (born between 1984 and 2002) who've been raised in the church will leave it sometime during the first decade of their adult lives. The cultural commitment to the church that has characterized American society from the beginning has fizzled, like a pop-bottle rocket reaching its zenith. A mere one-in-five Millennials believes "going to church is important." But those who affirm that they're actually growing spiritually point to their relationship with Jesus as one of their top-five drivers. And those who've bucked the generational trend and have stayed connected to church say there's one overriding factor in their ongoing commitment: "Jesus speaks to me in a personal and relevant way."[11] When Rachel Held Evans, one of the top 10 Christian bloggers online and a *New York Times* bestselling author, wrote "Why Millennials Are Leaving the Church" in July 2013, the piece sparked more than 100,000 social media reactions in its first week. The crux of her commentary is simple: "We're not leaving the church because we don't find the cool factor there; we're leaving the church because we don't find Jesus there. Like every generation before ours and every generation after, deep down, we long for Jesus."[12]

A deep, ongoing, intimate relationship with Jesus changes everything.

But when we are caught in the slow downward spiral of a tips-and-techniques mentality, a passionate relationship with Jesus is reduced to something a lot more transactional—something like a mid-marriage malaise.

We all know couples just like this—the current that flows through their union is carrying them, inexorably, into the Dead Sea:

- They eat together, but they chew in silence and stare off into space.
- Their eyes are no longer fixed on each other—the little screen in their hand is more fascinating.
- They're pleasant to each other, most of the time, but seem quick on the trigger when one or the other does that irritating thing they've been told a million times not to do.
- When one of them starts to tell a funny story, one that's been told one too many times, the other is quick to shoot the "not again" look.
- They sigh a lot around each other, and hardly ever touch each other.
- He heads down to his man-cave for poker or pay-per-view with the guys; she finds new and creative reasons to go shopping or drink wine at a watercolor painting party with the girls.
- They'd never admit it openly, but they believe there's nothing really new to learn about each other.
- The age of wonder is over, replaced by the age of resignation and disappointment: *"Darling, I want you to know that I'm committed to continue pacing the perimeter of the holding tank that is our relationship."*

We'd never *say* all we want out of our relationship with Jesus is a comfortable, predictable, unobtrusive way to live more happily, but we sure *act* like we do.

And with Jesus we say: "You have your space and I have mine—let's keep our relationship...manageable." We read the Bible, sometimes, but only when we feel guilty that we haven't read the Bible for a while. We feel a little better after we volunteer to serve meals at the homeless shelter for our church's "Service Saturday" outreach, but we quickly settle back into benign disinterest with Jesus a week or so later. Something the pastor says during his sermon blows on the embers of our relationship and we pray for the first time in weeks, but that emotional moment is quickly overshadowed by the argument we have with our teenage daughter on the way home from church, the bills we just remembered that we forgot to pay, and the season finale of our favorite reality show. Our "marriage" to Jesus is stuck in the rut of rote—we're just going through the motions. And, unconsciously, we're resigned to settle for our mid-marriage malaise with him. We'd never *say* all we want out of our relationship with Jesus is a comfortable, predictable, unobtrusive way to live more happily, but we sure *act* like we do.

But the Spirit of Jesus who lives in our hearts will not settle for this. He doesn't want the kind of relationship that slowly descends into tolerance, rote politeness, and comfortable deadness; he wants an epic romance that's full of daring risks, remarkable sacrifices, permeating joy, and long stretches of soul-satisfying intimacy. And that explains the unsettled feeling most of us have—something in the soul longs for the intimacy it was created to enjoy, and it is unwilling to acquiesce to a *transactional* relationship with God. We were created for something more, and Jesus' eccentric, passionate, and sometimes mystifying behavior points to it:

• He tells us that we must "eat his body and drink his blood" if we want "any part of him" (John 6).

• He describes the relationship he wants with us, metaphorically, like a branch abiding in a vine, like a groom's intimate relationship with his bride, like a sheep's desperate and dependent relationship with its shepherd, like two lovers who can't take their eyes off of each other.

• He has no problem asking his followers to give up everything for him, including their very lives.

• He expects many people will outright reject him—that's why he's ecstatic over those who go all-in with him. But he *can't stand* playing it safe; when people go halfway with him, he metaphorically spits them out of his mouth (Revelation 3:14-16).

Like any passionate lover, Jesus speaks the language of epic romance—a kind of raw intimacy that's embarrassing to talk about in polite company. When Christian songwriter John Mark McMillan wrote "How He Loves," one of the most popular worship songs of the last decade, he included this eye-opening stanza:

So heaven meets earth like a sloppy wet kiss
And my heart turns violently inside of my chest,
I don't have time to maintain these regrets,
When I think about the way…
He loves us
Oh! How He loves us…

Of course, if you've ever sung this song in church, that first line in the stanza may take you aback. It's in McMillan's original, but not in the version that's popular in most churches today. McMillan gave his permission to David Crowder, the renowned and respected singer/songwriter, to cover his song with this replacement line: *"So heaven meets earth like an unforeseen kiss…"*—and Crowder's edited version is now the one most people have heard. The reason he requested the lyric change, Crowder told McMillan, was "because he knew that there are literally thousands of people who would never hear the song the way it was." McMillan admits: "I knew it was only a matter of time before someone recorded a version with a different line." The reason, of course, is that "sloppy wet kiss" is a description that seems way too *sexual* for a worship song. McMillan wrote the song the day after his close friend was killed in a car accident—that's why his lyrics are so raw and intimate. Great pain produced a line in a worship song that frames our "heaven meets earth" relationship with God with a metaphor that suggests raw intimacy, and it made a lot of people uncomfortable.[13]

Switching genres and eras, an old Frank Sinatra song perfectly describes the cadence inside the heart of Jesus:

All or nothin' at all
Half a love never appealed to me
If your heart, it never could yield to me
Then I'd rather, rather have nothin' at all[14]

It is not how *we* describe the relationship that matters—what really matters is how *Jesus* describes it.

The Bible is many things: historical record, poetry, an ongoing narrative of redemption, and even a handbook for life. But what it is, centrally, is a firsthand account of an epic romance between God and his creation. In *Love and War*, authors John and Stasi Eldredge condense the meaning of life into one sentence: "We live in a great love story, set in the midst of war."[15] This romance, the way Jesus described it and lived it out, is far closer to a sloppy wet kiss reality than our church-ified standards typically allow. But it is not how *we* describe the relationship that matters—what really matters is how *Jesus* describes it.

You Will Go Free

Clearly, Jesus has ambitions for his relationship with us that obliterate our nice, pleasant descriptions of him. He wants it all—rather, *he wants us all, down to the grime under our dirty fingernails*. And when we respond to his longing by living a life that is more and more centered around him, we find release from the prison of our malaise and an invitation into an epic life that orbits around him the same way our attention stays fixed when we see for the first time Niagara Falls or the Grand Canyon or the Eagle Nebula or the inviting flutter of our beloved's eyelashes. Jesus' intentions fit well in the bedroom, not in a Rotary Club meeting. He's the *reality* behind the mythic poet/warrior our hearts have always longed for. And rebel singer/songwriter Tonio K's song "You Will Go Free" captures the missional purpose of that original Poet/Warrior, its message drilling down to the bedrock of our hearts:

You've been a prisoner, baby,
Been a prisoner all your life,
Held captive in an alien world where they hold your need for love to your
*   throat, like a knife,*
And they make you jump,
And they make you do tricks,
They take what started off such an innocent heart, and they break it, and break
*   it, and break it until it almost can't be fixed.*
Well, I don't know when and I don't know how,
I don't know how long it's gonna take,
I don't know how hard it will be, but I know you will go free.
Now you can call it the devil, call it the big lie,
Call it a fallen world, whatever it is, it ruins almost everything we try,
It's the sins of the fathers, yeah, and it's the choices we make,
It's people screaming without making a sound, from prison cells in paradise
*   where we're chained to our mistakes.*
And I don't know when, and I don't know how,
I don't know how much it's gonna cost you, probably everything,
I know you will go free.
You can't see a jailer, you can't see the bar,
You can't turn your head around fast enough, but it's everywhere you are,
It's all around you,
Everywhere you walk, these prison walls surround you.
But in the midst of all this darkness, yeah, in the middle of this night,
I see the truth cut through this curtain like a laser, like a pure and holy light,
And I know I can't touch you now, yeah, and I don't want to speak too soon,
But when we get sprung from out these cages, baby, God knows what
*   we might do.*
But I don't know when and I don't know how, yeah,
I don't know if you'll be leaving alone or you'll be leaving with me,
But I know you will go free,
I know the truth will set you free,
The truth about who you are,
Truth about who you were always meant to be,
Yeah,
You will go free.[16]

We are all captives—some of us have made peace with our jailers, sprucing up our cells as best we can and distracting ourselves from our sometimes bleak or boring reality by using media, money, and momentum to self-medicate. But some of us can't stop hungering and thirsting for freedom. Some of us have been yearning to discover what life could look like if we "get sprung from out these cages," because "God knows what we might do." Some of us feel like sheep in desperate need of a shepherd, or broken branches pining for the life of the Vine, or lovers who stay awake into the heart of the night, longing to see the familiar outline of our beloved walking through the darkened doorway.

It's not possible to understand and embrace the heart of Jesus if our approach to knowing him is characterized by casual interest or benign pursuit. The only practical way to understand and love Jesus is to go all-in with him. I can describe what water feels like until I'm as blue-in-the-face as a swimming pool, but you won't truly *understand* it until you take the plunge. True understanding is always experiential. And, in the case of Jesus, a little *doesn't* go a long way. In fact, a whole lot of Jesus doesn't even scratch the surface. He's the most fascinating, unpredictable, remarkable person who ever walked the earth. It's going to take time—a glorious lifetime—to probe his depths. But that's what we do when we're invited into relationship with fascinating people.

The conventional understanding of Jesus as a mystery that we're not meant to know in full is hogwash.

The conventional understanding of Jesus as a mystery that we're not meant to know in full is hogwash. Jesus came to be known, and to reveal the heart of his Father. In John's Gospel, the "disciple Jesus loved" makes this declaration: "No one has ever seen God. But the unique One, who is himself God, is near to the Father's heart. He has revealed God to us" (John 1:18, NLT). Jesus' intention is to invite us into knowing him at the deepest, most intimate levels we humans can achieve. He's not hiding from us. But he's also not throwing himself at us. He pursues us with passion, and he longs to be pursued with similar passion—it's that kind of pursuit that unlocks his mysteries. Wholehearted pursuit is intrinsic to all great loves. We don't make epic films about people who make measured commitments to pursue their milquetoast lover with halfhearted caution.

In a life that is centered on Jesus, the gravitational pull of his orbit, at some point, feels like a tractor beam.

In a life that is centered on Jesus, the gravitational pull of his orbit, at some point, feels like a tractor beam—we can't escape it, or him. If, as the Apostle Paul asserts, everything in the created world is a metaphor for "His invisible attributes, His eternal power and divine nature" (Romans 1:20), then maybe black holes exist to help us understand the magnetic effect of drawing near to Jesus. Just as a black hole's overwhelming mass creates a gravitational pull so strong that even light cannot escape it, the passionate pursuit of the real Jesus is our "event horizon"—as we draw nearer and nearer to him, we will cross an invisible boundary of his black-hole presence, from which no escape will be possible. We will be like Peter before us, who answered Jesus' plaintive question to his disciples: "You do not want to go away also, do you?" with his own black-hole response: "Lord, to whom shall we go?"(John 6:67-68).

Endnotes

1 "What Do We Really Know About Jesus?" by Bart D. Ehrman in the December 17, 2012, issue of *Newsweek*.

2 From a survey report by the Barna Group titled "Most American Christians Do Not Believe That Satan or the Holy Spirit Exist," published April 10, 2009.

3 From the raw footage of videotaped interviews of young adults across America, commissioned for a segment in the Group Magazine Live workshop tour.

4 You can get a good cross-section of these synonyms for "nice" in the entry "Famous People Describe Jesus," posted on JesusCentral.com—jesuscentral.com/ji/life-of-jesus-modern/jesus-famous.php.

5 Eugene Peterson, from the foreword for *Jesus Mean and Wild: The Unexpected Love of an Untamable God* by Mark Galli (Grand Rapids, MI: Baker Books), 11.

6 From my own transcription of Peter Kreeft's lecture "The Shocking Beauty of Jesus," given at Gordon-Conwell Seminary on September 20, 2007, and later expanded upon in his book *Jesus-Shock* (St. Augustine's Press, 2008).

7 *The Armstrong Lie* is a film directed by Alex Gibney, distributed by Sony Pictures Classics and released in 2013.

8 The entire text of "An Ordinary Man," by Thabiso Mohare, is reprinted as part of an "All Things Considered" report on December 13, 2013 (National Public Radio).

9 Results from the Pew Research Center's second U.S. Religious Landscape Study (released on May 12, 2015), a follow-up to its first comprehensive study of religion in America, conducted in 2007. Quote from CNN.com post "Millennials Leaving Church in Droves, Study Finds," by Daniel Burke (posted on May 12, 2015).

10 Scott Thumma, "A Health Checkup for U.S. Churches" by Hartford Institute for Religion Research (from a presentation at the Future of the Church Summit at Group Publishing, Loveland, CO, October 22, 2012).

11 From the Barna Research Group report "5 Reasons Millennials Stay Connected to the Church," released on September 27, 2013 (barna.org).

12 Rachel Held Evans, "Why Millennials Are Leaving the Church" blog entry posted on CNN.com's Belief Blog on July 27, 2013.

13 John Mark McMillan describes this story on his blog The Promenade, in a post titled "How He Loves, David Crowder, and Sloppy Wet Kisses," posted on September 14, 2009.

14 "All or Nothing at All" lyrics written by Dennis Matkosky, Jack Lawrence, Arthur Altman, Bobby Caldwell, and Dennis Matkowsky. Copyright: Universal-MCA Music Publishing, a Division of Universal Music Corp., Matkosky Music, Geffen Music, MCA Music Publishing A.D.O. Universal S.

15 John and Stasi Eldredge, *Love and War* (Doubleday Religion, 2009), 39.

16 Tonio K., "You Will Go Free," from the *Romeo Unchained* album (Gadfly Records, 1996), full song lyrics reprinted with permission.

2

Exploring the Lombardi Effect

"Perhaps nothing helps us make the movement from our little selves to a larger world than remembering God in gratitude. Such a perspective puts God in view in all of life, not just in the moments we set aside for worship or spiritual disciplines. Not just in the moments when life seems easy."

—Henri Nouwen

Vince Lombardi is widely regarded as the greatest pro football coach of all time. His Green Bay Packers teams are legendary—he produced five NFL championships in seven years and coached 11 Hall of Fame players. The NFL championship trophy is named after him. He's renowned for his demanding style of leadership, his insistence on perfection, and his passion for his players. That's why, after one forgettable practice that was marred by dropped passes and forgotten assignments, Lombardi showed up at that evening's team meeting in a foul mood. First, he railed on his players, insisting they still had a lot to learn. Then, dramatically, he thrust a football high above his head and bellowed: "We're starting at the beginning. Gentlemen, this is a football." Snarky bad-boy tight end Max McGee interrupted Lombardi to ask: "Coach, can you not go so fast?"[1]

Those of us who identify as Christian still need to be reminded of the Truth that undergirds every other truth—that Truth's name is Jesus.

Embedded in this now-iconic interchange is a persistent universal truth: We human beings are all notorious forgetters, and that's why world-class football players still need to be reminded of basic pigskin truths. It's also why those of us who identify as Christian still need to be reminded of the Truth that undergirds every other truth—that Truth's name is Jesus. When the Apostle Paul declared to the church at Corinth, "For I determined to know nothing among you except Jesus Christ, and Him crucified" (2 Corinthians 2:2), he was also metaphorically bellowing, "Gentlemen, this is a football."

Remembering to Remember

The key to Lombardi's staggering success as a football coach was directly tied to his dogged practice of helping his players remember the brutal realities of the game—then offering extravagant belief in them. He lived in the tension of the Stockdale Paradox. Hall of Fame guard Jerry Kramer recalls one heated interchange that became a tipping point in his career: "He gets up in my face, about six inches from my nose and gives me the concentration lecture, as in, 'The concentration period of a college student is five minutes, in high school it's three minutes, in kindergarten it's 30 seconds. And you don't even have that, mister. So where does that put you?' " After this diatribe, Kramer retreated to the locker room where he sat alone, his head slumped as he contemplated quitting football altogether. When Lombardi walked in, says Kramer, "He came over and patted me on the back. Then he tousled my hair. 'Son,' he said, 'don't you know that someday you're going to be the best guard in football?' That really got something started inside me."[2]

The people of God move through a remarkably predictable cycle—they stray, God gives them a dose of tough love, the people remember God, they return to faithfulness, they start forgetting, they stray...

Obviously, Lombardi was a tough-love coach—he was ferocious about the fundamentals because he understood the strong gravitational pull toward forgetting the obvious that leverages all human beings. And forgetting, it turns out, is destructive. In the season before Lombardi arrived, the Packers had a 1-10 record with five future Hall of Famers on the team. Their coach was disorganized, the players confused and unmotivated. They had forgotten how to play football—three of those five future stars contemplated quitting football completely. The season after Lombardi arrived, the team went 7-5 and he was named coach of the year. He reintroduced his team to the basics, helping them remember what was most important about the game and making them feel empowered to play at a high level. You see this same pattern of forgetting and its destructive consequences through the whole of the Bible. The people of God move through a remarkably predictable cycle—they stray, God gives them a dose of tough love, the people remember God, they return to faithfulness, they start forgetting, they stray... And the cycle repeats again and again. This dynamic is obvious in books such as Exodus, but it's a thread that runs through all of the Bible, and right down the center of our souls.

Because we are so prone to forget what is most basic and important about life, we need a steady stream of "Lombardi moments"—they represent the brutal reality of our human weakness. And our penchant to forget obvious things is not nearly as unusual as we suppose in our everyday lives. It's not too much of a stretch to say that all of us are born into a mild version of Alzheimer's, and our lives are merely a progression toward its acute stages as we get older. Dr. Leonard Guarente is director of MIT's Glenn Laboratory for the Science of Aging and the Novartis Professor of Biology. The moderator on a Big Think panel discussion asked Guarente, point-blank, if everyone should expect to get Alzheimer's if we simply live long enough. His answer was blunt: "It's certainly true that many, many people, maybe most people, would get Alzheimer's. So from a societal point of view, I think the answer is most people would be vulnerable."[3] This disease triggers an extreme and destructive form of forgetting—the profound loss of personal identity. It's an acute example of an everyday human reality, because we are all at risk of losing our sense of self when we forget the most basic truths that God is revealing to us in Jesus. Far from an intrusion into our normal stream of remembering, forgetting is intrinsic to our human experience. We are all infected with terminal forgetfulness—it's just a matter of degree.

The Apostle Paul understood this truth, and that his protégé, Timothy, would need his own concentration lecture. In his old age, and with the end of his life on the horizon, he offered this parting advice: "Remember Jesus Christ, raised from the dead, descended from David. This is my gospel, for which I am suffering even to the point of being chained like a criminal" (2 Timothy 2:8-9). Of course, Paul was tortured, beaten, and imprisoned because of his aggressive pursuit of Jesus. Timothy had lived through these beatings and shipwrecks and imprisonments with him—all for the glory and honor of Jesus. So why would Paul have to remind Timothy, a man whose whole life orbited around Jesus, about something as basic as the gospel? *Because he is humble enough to admit the truth: Everyone, including Paul, Timothy, John the Baptist, Peter, and the disciples—and now you and me—is a notorious forgetter.* Never assume the Jesus you think you know is the Jesus of reality. When you "eat or drink" him, the truth about who he is will quickly obliterate the taste of your false assumptions.

The Necessity of Discomfort

Paul uses the Greek word *mnemoneuo*, translated into English as "remember," to lead Timothy into his Lombardi moment. The word is in the present imperative tense, with a more literal meaning of "keep on remembering." And so, if we're to *keep on remembering Jesus*—the Jesus described and revealed by Scripture, not the Jesus of popular misconception—as a central way to grow spiritually and grow our impact in the world, then *forgetting* is our greatest enemy. And that's a problem, because most of us are way, way too comfortable and satisfied in our knowledge and understanding and experience of Jesus. That's why discomfort has such powerful leverage in our remembering. Pain and dissonance have the power to expose our determination to live our lives independent from Jesus. In the context of Jesus' well-known sheep/shepherd metaphor, as long as the sheep (that's us) have convinced themselves they have everything under control, they're not that interested in depending on their Good Shepherd (that's Jesus). But we know that the more *on top of things* the sheep think they are, the more exposed they are to danger, because they'll be less interested in listening to and obeying their Shepherd and more committed to fighting their own (impossible-to-win) battles.

Most of us are way, way too comfortable and satisfied in our knowledge and understanding and experience of Jesus.

Remember the "What Would Jesus Do?" movement, based on Charles Sheldon's classic book *In His Steps*? Years ago it was *really* big. The central question people were asking themselves was simple: *If Christians are supposed to be following Jesus, why aren't they making more of an impact in their daily lives?* The movement's answer was to imagine what everyday life might be like if all of us simply talked and acted more like Jesus. Well, that *would* change everything—especially if we took a Chipotle burrito, blessed it, and fed a stadium full of people with it. But, by any measure, the WWJD movement *didn't* change everything. The problem was the premise: Instead of encouraging people to *remember* Jesus as he really is, the movement prodded people to *imagine* Jesus as he's never been.

The less you know the truth about Jesus, the more likely you are to make a mistake when you try to imagine his behavior in your particular circumstances.

It's fine to imagine what *we think* Jesus might do when a friend betrays us or the MRI reveals bad news or the poser in the cubicle next to us gets the promotion we were hoping for, but the whole thing desperately depends on how well we *really know* the true Jesus, doesn't it? The less you know the truth about Jesus, the more likely you are to make a mistake when you try to imagine his behavior in your particular circumstances. Paul follows "keep on remembering" with a shotgun blast of the basic truths about Jesus (in 2 Timothy 2): "…raised from the dead, descended from David." Here he identifies Jesus by his past, present, and future. He is descended from the line of King David, as all the Old Testament prophecies about the coming Messiah asserted. And he is raised from the dead, marking the reality that Jesus was crucified, buried, and brought to life again—this is his present and future reality. This is Paul's pinpoint starting place—the thrust of the football above his head.

Keep On Seeking

If the Christian life we're living—a life that is, by definition, focused on following Jesus—is actually disconnected from who Jesus really is, we're likely headed for disillusionment and even despair. Our prevailing hope, remember, is fueled by our willingness to embrace brutal realities. A false reality about Jesus leads to a false hope about our lives. *And we can miss Jesus entirely by arrogantly assuming that our imagined responses to a partially understood Jesus mean that we're really following Jesus.*

So how can we make sure we don't miss Jesus? One Old Testament prophet tells us that we'll find God when we earnestly look for him (Jeremiah 29:13), and Jesus himself tells us we'll find him if we earnestly seek him: "Keep on asking, and you will receive what you ask for. Keep on seeking, and you will find. Keep on knocking, and the door will be opened to you" (Matthew 7:7, NLT). It's our determination to pursue Jesus, to embrace the truth about him, that unlocks our "remembering."

The Trinity is replacing a broken humanity's cycle of forgetting with a kingdom-of-God cycle of remembering.

Our trajectory in life is wholly dependent on our perception of God, and our perception of God is primarily dependent on the words and actions and teachings of Jesus. Of course, Jesus has come to rescue us from our bondage to sin and redeem us from slavery to our destructive whims. But Jesus has also come to remind us of the God we cannot see. In turn, the Holy Spirit has come to empower us to keep on remembering Jesus every moment of our lives. The Trinity is replacing a broken humanity's cycle of forgetting with a kingdom-of-God cycle of remembering. The Holy Spirit reminds us

of Jesus, and Jesus reminds us of his Father, and the Father, in tu
pointing to his Son. While Peter, James, and John jabber aw..., ----
on the Mount of Transfiguration, the bellowing voice of God intrudes into
their cycle of forgetting and kick-starts a cycle of remembering in them:
"This is My beloved Son, with whom I am well-pleased; listen to Him!"
(Matthew 17:5).

Even the disciples, who know Jesus in the flesh, don't really *know* him.
In John 14 Jesus is having a heart-to-heart with his closest friends, letting
them know it won't be long before he's gone from them. He tries to offer
comfort by reminding them that they "know the way where I am going."
But Thomas, confused, responds: "Lord, we do not know where You are
going, how do we know the way?" The disciples, like us, are a little thick.
They don't yet understand that Jesus is not offering them a new way of
living—he's offering them the chance to be *one* with him. He is not pointing
to the way into the kingdom of God; he is himself that way. And this is
why Jesus tells Thomas: "I am the way, and the truth, and the life; no one
comes to the Father but through Me. If you had known Me, you would
have known My Father also; from now on you know Him, and have seen
Him" (John 14:6-7).

Of course, the reality of what Jesus is saying is too fantastical to grasp,
even though Jesus has made no secret of who he claims to be. Philip,
desperate to somehow close the gap between his belief and unbelief, says,
"Lord, show us the Father, and it is enough for us." And here Jesus gets
positively, brutally, specific:

Have I been so long with you, and yet you have not come to know Me,
Philip? He who has seen Me has seen the Father; how can you say, "Show
us the Father"? Do you not believe that I am in the Father, and the Father
is in Me? The words that I say to you I do not speak on My own initiative,
but the Father abiding in Me does His works. Believe Me that I am in the
Father and the Father is in Me (John 14:9-11).

Jesus is perfectly living out a perfect reflection of the perfect God we can't see. And the reason this is so difficult for the disciples to accept is that they don't have (at least, not yet) something we have: the gift of the Holy Spirit, whose job description is to reveal the heart and true identity of Jesus. Remembering is hard enough for all of us on the road to Alzheimer's, but it would be impossible without the Spirit's ongoing, moment-by-moment impetus to help us keep on remembering. If we will invite him, the Spirit will replace our ill-conceived misconceptions about Jesus with the truth about him, down to the most intimate inclinations in his heart.

Jesus is perfectly living out a perfect reflection of the perfect God we can't see.

In his High Priestly Prayer (John 17), Jesus tells his Father out loud, with his disciples gathered near and listening, that he's accomplished everything he's been given to do, and that things are about to get better for his friends because *he's about to leave.* Why is he praying out loud, and why would he speak so positively about leaving his followers? I'd rather be with the people I love than away from them. But here Jesus clearly can't wait to leave—he knows that when he does, the people he loves will "get" him more fully than they have so far. He wants them (and us) to know that when he hands the baton to the Holy Spirit, our longing to know him more deeply will be possible. Like the woman at the well outside the city walls of Sychar, the Spirit makes it possible for us to take a long drink of Jesus' living water.

On the road to Emmaus, a few days after the crucifixion of Jesus and his reported resurrection has electrified Jerusalem, two of his disciples prove that much of what the Good Shepherd Jesus tried to get across to his sheep hadn't really stuck. They'd heard him, lived with him, and watched him, but they hadn't yet been transformed by him. We know this, because an incognito Jesus approaches them on the road and asks them to explain everything that's happened—their summation reveals their ignorance: "But we were hoping that it was He who was going to redeem Israel" (Luke 24:21). Jesus' response begins in verse 25 with a blunt diagnosis: "O foolish men and slow of heart to believe in all that the prophets have spoken!"

And then he narrates the story of God's redemptive plan from beginning to end, carried out and fulfilled first by his own submission to death, and then by his conquering of it—"Gentlemen, this is a football."

The Spirit makes it possible for us to move from *knowing about* Jesus to *knowing* Jesus.

As long as Jesus remains an *outside* influence, not an *inside* reality, we will struggle to understand and trust him. And that's why the Holy Spirit is the greatest gift we'll ever receive. The Spirit makes it possible for us to move from *knowing about* Jesus to *knowing* Jesus. This is knowing in the biblical sense—it's our most intimate act. And it has nothing at all to do with gathering bits of facts and trivia or ticking off a list of religious habits on our spiritual to-do list. This knowing isn't inviting our head; it's inviting our heart.

Endnotes

1 John Eisenberg, *That First Season: How Vince Lombardi Took the Worst Team in the NFL and Set It on the Path to Glory* (New York, NY: Mariner Books, 2010), 102.

2 From the online article "Leader of Men" by Mike Puma, published on ESPN.com.

3 From the transcript of a Big Think panel discussion "Will Everyone Get Alzheimer's If They Live Long Enough?" published on BigThink.com in 2011.

3

Rejecting the Culture of Should

"The kingdom of heaven is not come even when God's will is our law: it is come when God's will is our will. While God's will is our law, we are but a kind of noble slaves; when his will is our will, we are free children."

—George MacDonald

On Christmas Day, the pastor of a church on the East Coast posted this on his church's Facebook page:

We had a wonderful celebration of Jesus' birth last evening, with almost one hundred of us gathered together. It was, however, disappointing that some excused themselves from being there for secular and family celebrations that in reality had nothing to do with Christmas. If we are followers of Jesus we need to celebrate God coming among us in the faith community. The only legitimate excuse to be absent is if we are either in intensive care or the morgue. Is it any wonder that the event of Christ's birth has been reduced to an eggnog-and-cookies "Holiday" (replacing "Holy" day) celebration, when even those who say they are Christians fail to gather for the feast? Folks, it always comes down to our priorities and our level of commitment to living out our Baptismal Promises. If you made the wrong choice this Christmas, reflect deeply on how you can change it, and why you should. Jesus is God's love in the flesh, and the only response he seeks from us is for us to return that love! Why would we ever miss the birthday celebration for someone we love and who loves us?[1]

This pastor, of course, has just shoveled a steaming pile of *should* into the lap of his congregation. It's an extreme example, yes, but somewhere along the way you've almost certainly been similarly *shoulded-on* by a church leader or a well-meaning friend or a television preacher or even your parents. The message, blatant or subtle, is always that we *should* love Jesus because, well, we *should*—it's our *duty* to love Jesus. We're supposed to shoulder the weight of our "Baptismal Promises" like a cross-shaped yoke. But this *should*-yoke was never Jesus' idea; rather he specifically described his "yoke" as an attractive option for anyone who is "weary and heavy-laden" and in need of rest: "Take my yoke upon you and learn from Me, for I am gentle and humble in heart, and you will find rest for your souls. For My yoke is easy and My burden is light" (Matthew 11:28-30).

Well, I'd like to apologize on behalf of the church for that—Jesus isn't trying to *should* you into loving him.

Not long ago I was standing in front of a roomful of college students—all of them summer-staffers who were about to spend two months on the road setting up and leading week-long Group Mission Trip experiences for teenagers. My role during their two weeks of training in the Colorado mountains was to lead the opening-day morning and evening devotion times. Toward the end of that first night's gathering, I looked out on a sea of eager college-age faces and suddenly got choked up. The Spirit of Jesus was poking at me. So I paused and said, with gravity, "I want to apologize to all of you on behalf of the church." The room suddenly got very quiet. "I know most of you have grown up in the church," I continued, "and your whole life you've been told you should love Jesus because…you *should* love Jesus. Well, I'd like to apologize on behalf of the church for that—Jesus isn't trying to *should* you into loving him. That's our misguided strategy, not his. Jesus wants to invite you to know him much more deeply. If you will respond to that invitation, let's see how that impacts your love for him."

I had tears running down my face as I said these words; but I saw tears running down the faces of those college students, too. Their hearts craved so much more than the *shoulded* relationship with Jesus they'd been force-fed their whole lives. The yoke of Jesus is an invitation to enter into his love—and when we are yoked to Jesus, he tells us the primary (and counter-church-culture) effect will be rest for our souls.

A Heresy Incognito

It's wrong to should people into a love relationship, and it's worse than wrong—actually, heretical—to should people into a love relationship with Jesus. A heresy is a twisted truth. Only a person who identifies as a Christian can say or do something heretical; by definition, you have to believe in something before you can turn it into a twisted belief. And the Apostle Paul assured Timothy that a whole lot of heresy was coming down the pike toward us: "For a time is coming when people will no longer listen to sound and wholesome teaching. They will follow their own desires and will look for teachers who will tell them whatever their itching ears want to hear. They will reject the truth and chase after myths" (2 Timothy 4:3-4, NLT).

Heretical shoulds represent the myths we're chasing, because we falsely believe they lead to worship, or a more committed relationship with Jesus. The shoulding motivation is always pushing us toward religious imperatives—the determined do's and don'ts of what passes for our spiritual life—and we have a love/hate relationship with them. Here's a bracing reality: Some part of us would prefer to live in a spirit of duty, because we can do that on autopilot. It's the sort of thing our itching ears want to hear. It's a lot easier to merely *serve* your beloved than to unconditionally love her or him. It's a kind thing when I make sure to switch on the coffee pot just before my wife gets up or when I carry the groceries in from the car, but it's hardly risky. Following should-laws offers a twisted comfort, but it's short-lived. Counselor and author Steve Merritt says: "Laws put us in the driver's seat for a moment. We briefly—and falsely—receive the earthly acceptance we crave. But the Law creates only two kinds of people: Pharisees and failures."[2] Even more, if my love for my wife is reduced to kind acts of service, I've subtly traded an epic opportunity to risk my vulnerability for a safe and cautious "measurable." And when I make this trade, I ignore the one thing that really matters.

In Luke's Gospel account, Jesus is traveling through Bethany when he's invited to dine in the home of his friends Mary and Martha. While Martha does what hostesses are expected to do for their last-minute guests, scrambling to prepare food and refreshments, Mary ignores the clamor (and her responsibilities) so she can sit at the feet of Jesus. And Martha, just as you and I would likely do, blows a gasket: "Lord, do You not care that my sister has left me to do all the serving alone? Then tell her to help me." Jesus' response undermines Martha's hanging religious imperative: "Martha, Martha, you are worried and bothered about so many things; but only a few things are necessary, really only one, for Mary has chosen the good part, which shall not be taken away from her" (Luke 10:38-42).

People who gravitate to duty in their relationship with God prefer to keep him at a respectable distance. They'd rather follow orders than follow their heart.

But another part of us hates trading the hope of true intimacy for the drudgery of rote obedience. We long for Cinderella to be discovered by her prince, because she won't be a slave to her evil stepmother's whims any longer. And that's why a life of shoulding, with the inherent promise that it will put us in the driver's seat, sometimes makes us sick to our stomach. I got married when I was 29—a little late in my prime hunting season, so to speak. What if my parents, worried I was destined for a lifetime of humming the chorus to Gilbert O'Sullivan's "Alone Again, Naturally," decided to do the heavy lifting for me? What if they'd knocked on my door one night and I'd opened it to find them standing there with a woman I'd known in college, but not very well? And what if they said: "Hey, we've found someone we think is perfect for you—we've checked her out and we're a hundred percent sure you should love her"? And what if, during this long and awkward encounter on my doorstep, my parents grew increasingly insistent about this woman's obvious matrimonial qualifications, and increasingly frustrated by my reluctance to get in lock-step with their should?

That's right—*yuck*. We're just not wired by God this way. Jesus doesn't want a "supposed-to" relationship with us. He doesn't want to be that girl, standing on my doorstep, listening to my parents convince me into loving her. He wants to be known and loved for who he is, and the only way that's going to happen is for us to slow down and get to know his heart. Have we really soaked in the personality of Jesus—pursued him as the most fascinating, magnetic, lightning-bolt person who ever lived? And if he's really all that incredible, why are supposed-tos even necessary? People who are caught up in a romantic relationship don't have to be told to focus on the object of their affection; it's hard to stop thinking about the person, actually. No matter what we're doing or who we're with, our thoughts stray to the object of our passion. And that's not because we *should* be preoccupied with the object of our affection—we simply can't help ourselves, because we're inexorably drawn to beauty.

Jesus wants to capture our hearts, not force our obedience.

The Sin of the Pharisees

My pastor and close friend, Tom Melton, has thrown many "Tom-isms" at me over the years that have changed the way I think about my relationship with Jesus. One of them is a real scalpel of an insight: "We don't really believe Jesus is beautiful; otherwise, we wouldn't describe our relationship with him as so much work." Let that one cut through the heresy of should. We'd never buy a Valentine's Day card that read: "It Sure Takes a Lot of Work to Love You!" But the church has often, albeit unwittingly, framed our relationship with Jesus as a sort-of long slog through the land of religious imperative—a life characterized by nose-to-the-grindstone duty, not sloppy wet kisses.

We'd never buy a Valentine's Day card that read: "It Sure Takes a Lot of Work to Love You!"

This is exactly why Jesus was so persistently hard on the Pharisees and teachers of the law. These were people who had constructed an entire identity around their ability to adhere to and propagate an ever-growing list of shoulds. They were aficionados of religious imperatives, always finding new and creative ways to require greater fealty to a lengthening list of God-duties. And their systemized, check-the-box approach to a relationship with God disgusted Jesus. He had zero patience for the shoulding way of life. Summing up the Pharisees' heresy, he tells his disciples: "They tie up heavy burdens, and lay them on men's shoulders; but they themselves are unwilling to move them with so much as a finger" (Matthew 23:4). The "heavy burdens" he's referencing have the same DNA as the Facebook-posting pastor's insistence that "the only legitimate excuse to be absent is if we are either in intensive care or the morgue."

Intimacy between God and his creation is abhorrent to Satan, and shoulds have proven to be his most effective intimacy-killers.

Jesus came to fulfill a prophetic job description, first uttered 500 years earlier by Isaiah, the booming messenger of God, in a specific reference to the coming Messiah: "[The Lord] has sent Me to proclaim release to the captives" (Luke 4:18, quoting Isaiah 61:1). The bars of our prison cell, so carefully guarded by the Pharisees and all those who live in their spirit, are the shame-based rules and regulations of a "try harder to get better" mentality. It's a system that Satan, the enemy of God, not only approves of, but persistently advocates. The one thing he hates most—the thing that violates his sensibilities and shocks his standards—is the "sloppy wet kiss" God's children offer their "Abba." Intimacy between God and his creation is abhorrent to Satan, and shoulds have proven to be his most effective intimacy-killers.

Taste and See

If we're exhausted by our own long list of shoulds in life, then the misguided church's supplemental list of impossible-to-master shoulds only magnifies our weariness. The good news, of course, is that Jesus is not interested in shoulding us into an obedient relationship with him. Rather, the way forward is prophetically highlighted by King David, a man after God's own heart, in this line from one of his epic poems: "O taste and see that the Lord is good; how blessed is the man who takes refuge in Him!" (Psalm 34:8). Because we're tasting things all the time, we forget what an intimate thing it is to do. To bite into something and swallow requires that we take an outside thing and make it an inside thing. To fully taste we must ingest. And in a way, ingesting something into our body is at least as intimate as our sexual behaviors. We have stripped tasting of its true intimacy by over-familiarity—but imagine what it took for the first person in history to put something into his mouth to taste it. What would it take for us to reclaim the wonder of that primal experience when we're "tasting" Jesus?

In the history of civilization, there have been only 227 people in the world who have earned the designation "Master Sommelier."

In the history of civilization, there have been (as of the moment I write this) only 227 people in the world who have earned the designation "Master Sommelier." A sommelier is, literally, a wine steward—a highly trained expert who is skilled at offering detailed recommendations for food pairings with wine varietals and vintages. The reason so few have earned this honor is that the three-day test to become a "Master Somm" is so difficult that only the radically all-in are able to pass it. Candidates endure a challenging oral examination on the theory of wine-making, a practical evaluation of their ability to interact with customers and serve their wine needs, and (most daunting) a blind tasting of six wines—"within twenty-five minutes he or she must...identify, where appropriate, grape varieties, country of origin, district and appellation of origin, and vintages of the wines tasted."[3] Watching candidates practice for this part of the test is like watching someone build, in their backyard, a rocket that can take them to the moon and back. They have roughly four minutes to taste, study, and smell the bouquet of each wine and then describe it exactly, down to the winery that produced it. It looks impossible, unless you've dedicated every fiber of yourself to tasting the subtle nuances of wine.[4]

The trouble is, when we realize the "all-in" it takes for anyone to be incredible at anything, we most often think "I could never do that" or "These people are crazy-committed to this thing." The sacrifice and passion and perseverance it takes to become a master at anything can seem daunting for normal people. So are the people we call saints simply the Master Somms of the Christian life—the crazy-committed ones? Well, in the first century, *anyone* who made a commitment to follow Jesus was commonly called a saint. In the book of Romans, it's Paul's favorite way to refer to his brothers and sisters in Christ. Is it possible *every single one of us* can live a Master Somm lifestyle with Jesus, tasting him so often and so deeply that we know his intimate nooks and crannies? Well, Jesus not only invites us into this kind of relationship with him, he tells us it is our *only* path to life: "Truly, truly, I say to you, unless you eat the flesh of the Son of Man and drink His blood, you have no life in yourselves" (John 6:53). If we're going to experience Jesus so intimately that it's like eating and drinking him, we'll naturally end up crazy-committed to him.

When we enter into refuge, we go inside our protector.

To taste Jesus is to invite him from our outside to our inside—to bring life itself into our "dying branch." And when we feast on the Son of God, David reminds us, we also take refuge in him—the Hebrew word translated "refuge" in Psalm 34:8 means "to flee for protection." When we enter into refuge, we go inside our protector. Jesus describes the kind of relationship the Trinity is aiming for in his impassioned conversation with his Father just before he is betrayed, scourged, and crucified: "I pray that they will all be one, just as you and I are one—as you are in me, Father, and I am in you. And may they be in us so that the world will believe you sent me" (John 17:21, NLT). Jesus wants Master Somm–style lovers...people who will first risk a little taste of him, then tip the rim a bit more, then drain the glass and reach for more. A little taste leads to a bigger taste, and pretty soon we're uncorking Jesus all the time—our whole lives are spent feasting and drinking at his table: "Go therefore to the main highways, and as many as you find there, invite to the wedding feast" (Matthew 22:9).

An "in us" relationship with Jesus is a feast of body and blood—a gathering of Master Somms—and it has nothing to do with shoulding. It does, however, have everything to do with sheep and pigs.

Endnotes

1 From a December 25, 2014, post on a New York church's Facebook page. I have intentionally withheld names.

2 Steve Merritt, "Personal Growth" column titled "Job's Friends," published in the Fall 2015 issue of *Group Magazine*.

3 From the website The Court of Master Sommeliers (mastersommeliers.org), described in the "Courses and Schedules" section.

4 From the documentary *Somm*, written and directed by Jason Wise (Forgotten Man Films, 2013).

Living a Sheep's Life

"We cannot be loved without being changed. When people experience love, they begin to grow lovely."

—John Ortberg

Jesus repeatedly describes the people of God as sheep. In John 10 he calls himself the "shepherd of the sheep" and insists that his sheep hear his voice when he calls them by name, and that the sheep follow him because they know his voice. And, he promises, he fully intends to lay down his life for the sheep, not like a hireling who will leave the sheep and flee when a wolf threatens them. He concludes his metaphoric exploration into sheep-i-ness with this declaration: "I know My own, and My own know Me" (John 10:14). Later, sheep are the focal point of his last conversation on earth—when he walks the beach on the Sea of Galilee with Peter, telling this professional fisherman three times to "feed my sheep" as his parting exclamation point. Shepherd is his favorite metaphor for himself, and sheep is his favorite metaphor for everyone else.

It's so important to pay better attention to the metaphors Jesus chooses—to discover the remarkable meaning in their detail.

Jesus habitually teaches and exhorts using metaphors, because the realities he's trying to convey about the kingdom of God require translation. A metaphor connects a thing we don't understand all that well with something that is very familiar to us, so that we can understand its heart. People who are described as lemmings follow others indiscriminately; diners who eat too fast are pigs; and children who are growing into adulthood are blooming, for example. And Jesus can convey infinite meaning in his metaphors because he is the master of language and imagination—our ability to wield words compared to his ability is the difference between a butter knife and a broadsword. So when Jesus uses a metaphor, it's always a perfect metaphor. That means we can drill into the meaning of it, deeper and deeper, as we learn the metaphor's nuances. And that's why it's so important to pay better attention to the metaphors Jesus chooses—to discover the remarkable meaning in their detail. But when we do that with "sheep," recognizing that Jesus has perfectly chosen this particular animal to describe our reality, it's a humiliating exploration. Sheep are...

• timid, fearful, and easily panicked;

• slow-witted and gullible;

• vulnerable to fear, frustration, pests, and hunger;

• easily prodded into a stampede—they're quick to descend into a mob mentality;

• without means of self-defense, and easily killed by their many natural predators if left unprotected;

• jealous and competitive for dominance;

• always seeking fresh water and fresh pastures, but lacking discernment in their choices;

• stubborn, always insisting on their own way;

• unable to right themselves when tipped onto their backs;

• highly agitated if someone tries to clean or shear their wool;

• creatures of habit that often get stuck in ruts; and

• needy—they require more diligent care than any other breed of livestock.

It's hard to stomach this list, because we generally have such a high opinion of ourselves, and sheep are, well, embarrassing. Wouldn't a metaphoric lion or eagle or (if we have to settle) even a cow more accurately describe our default identity? But hiding in the shadow of our overblown ego is our sheep-ish reality—it's not all that difficult to see ourselves described in these bullet points.

He wants to shepherd us because he loves us to death—a literal truth.

Jesus loves his brutal-reality metaphors—but he is never denigrating us when he compares us to sheep. Notice the prevailing hope embedded in this description: "When [Jesus] saw the crowds, he had compassion on them, because they were harassed and helpless, like sheep without a shepherd" (Matthew 9:36, NIV). Yes, we are sheep, but we have a Shepherd who loves us and will defend us. The deepest truth about our sheep-i-ness is summed up in a well-known lyric from a children's song: "Jesus loves me, this I know." He wants to shepherd us because he loves us to death—a literal truth.

His promise to lay down his life for the sheep is not a poetic flourish. In John 10, when Jesus describes himself as "the door of the sheep," he means that no wolf can get at us without going through him. At night, a shepherd who owns his own herd will stretch his body across the opening of his sheep-pen and go to sleep. A hireling will not. The symbol we use to identify ourselves as Christians could as easily be a sheepgate as a cross, because the story of Jesus nailed to a cross is also the story of a Good Shepherd—an owner, not a hireling—protecting the opening of God's sheep pen from a wolf with his own body.

The Currency of Trust

We sheep don't need a better understanding of how to avoid getting eaten by wolves; rather, we need a deeper trust in and obedience to our tender/fierce Shepherd, who will look out for us, defend us, and rescue us. In a world where many of us struggle to fit in, we fit perfectly in our Good Shepherd's pen. He wants us. And he knows we need him, because we have an abysmal track record of shepherding ourselves. But our inability to trust him wholeheartedly—to forget about fending for ourselves and, instead, submit to him—is directly tied to our shallow and inaccurate understanding of his heart. Trust is the organic fruit that grows when we've tasted the goodness and faithfulness of another's heart.

My family doesn't watch a lot of television, but we do watch the Emmy-winning reality show *The Amazing Race* together. The show's producers are the circus masters for an around-the-world competition that requires two-person teams to face physical, mental, and emotional challenges to win. In one episode set in New Zealand, contestants had to lead a herd of sheep through a series of challenges and barriers and then into a small pen. Initially, every one of the teams made the same mistake—they tried to chase or intimidate the sheep into going where they wanted them to go, which always led to a chaotic, bleat-y disaster. But a few of the teams discovered, early on, how to build trust with their sheep—they approached them with calm strength and a gentle voice, then *invited* them into the pen. Those teams that continued to use a panicky, dominating, and aggressive approach exhausted themselves into hopelessness. The teams that used an approach characterized by non-anxious strength quickly succeeded.[1]

The visionary rabbi/educator/counselor/business strategist Edwin Friedman, in his masterwork on leadership *A Failure of Nerve*, says the key to influencing healthy change in any relational environment is "bringing our non-anxious presence"[2] into every situation. He means that catalytic leaders bring profound change to their organizations because of their *orientation*, not because of their rhetoric. People are more influenced by whatever our life orbits around—the center of our life's solar system—than by our words. It's the essence of a person—the way we experience his or her core personality—that relaxes us or makes us anxious; that inspires us or makes us cautious; that invites us or repels us. Think about the people who've had the biggest impact for good in your life. What are their common characteristics? These descriptions fit the people I'm thinking of right now: relaxed strength, determination, congruence, regulated ferocity, surprising pursuit, a willingness to lead, and a self-security that allows them to unabashedly enjoy others. Do these descriptions resonate for you, too?

In general, our words do little to affect real change, but our catalytic *presence* does a lot.

In general, our words do little to affect real change, but our catalytic *presence* does a lot. This means it's more important to understand and trust the *heart* of a person than it is to trust that person's *ideas and strategies*. When we invite strong, trustworthy, and differentiated people into our lives, we always change for the better. Differentiated people will not slavishly obey the external forces that are trying to mold them—their source of life and security and identity comes from God, not from the leveraging voices that press in on them. Sheep won't obey what they don't trust. They can sense weakness and worry in their leaders and they're frightened by it, so they'll refuse to obey them. Conversely, they're easily influenced by strength and calm and a relaxed firmness. This is why it's so crucial that we get a better, longer, deeper taste of the heart of Jesus. Our fixation on tips-and-techniques that are drawn from the teachings of Jesus can actually keep us from trusting him more deeply, because we're memorizing and attempting to cook up his recipes, not learning to appreciate his heart. The recipes are fantastic—but it's the heart that really matters.

The Medium Is the Message

All of us experience seasons of emotional and psychological darkness. A few years ago I faced a distinctly challenging season, brought on by profound relational losses, suffocating pressures at work, health problems in my family, and financial stresses. Any one of those things would have been difficult for me to face, but all of them arriving on my doorstep together was like finding the entire cast of *The Sopranos* waiting for me on my porch. By mid-summer, I was in a dark and disorienting place, and I couldn't pull myself out of it. Of course, my wife and my kids knew I was struggling, but they didn't know that I was descending into hopelessness. Then, on a warm July night, Jesus parachuted behind enemy lines and invaded my world.

I went to our mailbox that night to grab our daily dose of bills and flyers, and instead found a little white box with my name and address typed on a label, but no return address or postage. Curious, I opened the box before I went back inside—there was nothing in it but a tiny figure of Phineas from the Disney Channel cartoon *Phineas and Ferb,* and a short note that ended with an encouraging Scripture passage. Wow, I thought, whoever sent this to me knows that I love *Phineas and Ferb* and watch it with my daughter Emma. There was no marking of any kind on the box and nothing to identify the sender. Immediately, I began brainstorming possible suspects. Once inside I showed my whole family the box and its contents, and they were quickly caught up in the mystery. I didn't know this was only the tip of the iceberg.

Every week for seven weeks I received another little white box in our mailbox—same typed-out label, along with another little figure from *Phineas and Ferb* and an elaborate and encouraging note. My circle of suspects increased as I asked friends and family members if they were responsible for this affirmation assault, and each one insisted they had nothing to do with it. Most had never even heard of *Phineas and Ferb*. My daughters and my wife were equally obsessed with the mystery, maybe even more than I was. It became a nightly game around our dinner table for each of us to throw out the names of potential masterminds behind this plot and then build a case for their "guilt." Each delivery was clearly intended to encourage me and frame my life experience in a hopeful scriptural context. And, initially, it was exciting to open the mailbox every week and find another box waiting for me. But I didn't tell anyone my secret: I knew these secretive gifts were supposed to lift my spirits and give me hope, *but they did nothing to change my emotional reality.*

Sometimes the encouragement we get isn't the encouragement we demand.

Sometimes the encouragement we get isn't the encouragement we demand. I mean, others' best efforts to offer us a hand up out of our emotional cesspool simply aren't enough. And it's embarrassing and even shameful to admit this truth—that's why I kept my real feelings hidden. I'd feign excitement every time a box arrived, and I continued to pursue the culprits, but I was slipping further down into the cesspool, not scrambling out of it. Jesus says: "If then the light that is in you is darkness, how great is the darkness!" (Matthew 6:23). I was living this truth.

In the eighth week I went to the mailbox and there was no box. Instead, I found a plain white envelope with the same carefully typed label and no return address or postage. I opened the envelope and read this:

Dear Rick,

Sadly, there are going to be no more Phineas and Ferb characters coming in the mail. We hope they gave you a lot of encouragement and helped you keep going. We hope you had as much fun with it as we did. We all need a little mystery in our lives. By doing this we just wanted to let you know that we care about you and that we believe in you. God is watching out for you and always knows best. If you fully rely on him you will have nothing to worry about.

Even though we won't be sending any more verses we want you to keep going and to enjoy every moment of your life. You are an amazing person who has affected so many other lives; don't forget that. We still can't believe you haven't figured out it's us yet. We really thought it would be harder to fool you! Because you seem so interested in knowing who we are, we will give you one chance to find out. Once you get this letter we will give you 24 hours to figure out who we are. We promise, we will tell you the truth. The only rules to this game are, you cannot ask other people's opinions. You have to figure this out without the help of others. If you don't guess correctly in 24 hours, we will never reveal ourselves. (We really do mean it!) The clue we will give you is this: the second person involved has never successfully kept a secret until now. He/she rose to the occasion.

Again, we hope you had a lot of fun and now have many funny stories to tell! Good luck, keep going, and enjoy life! (There is a verse down below, it's a little long but it is really encouraging.)

Sincerely, Unanimous

(Followed by a Scripture passage from Matthew 6:25-34 that begins: "Therefore I tell you, do not worry about your life...")

Clearly, this final note was not only profound, but it also gave our search for the mastermind a deadline. And whoever it was, I did know one thing—"Unanimous" is an interesting variation on "Anonymous." My wife and I spent lunch throwing out possibilities all over again, but I knew I just wasn't going to figure this out—we'd exhausted every one of our possibilities. And, more troubling, I'd become emotionally numb to it all. Nothing about the note touched me in any way.

Later that afternoon I was in my home office with my wife, running through our list of usual suspects one more time as my daughter Emma sat in front of the computer, doing her homework. On a whim, more as a joke than a serious question, I asked Emma if she was actually the *Phineas and Ferb* bandit. I'd never even considered the possibility that my daughters were involved in this scheme, because it was so elaborate and they seemed genuinely shocked and delighted by each new delivery. So I didn't turn to look at Emma when I asked the question. She paused a little before she answered, and I swiveled around in my chair to look at her. "Emma," I demanded, "look at me—you're not the *Phineas and Ferb* bandit, are you?" She was quick to deny it, but she couldn't hide an ever-so-slight grin. And then an impossible possibility gripped me: Could my two daughters, at that time 9 and 13, have planned and carried out this massive operation all on their own? My jaw dropped as the truth set in—I couldn't speak. My older daughter Lucy was due to get off the bus at that moment, so I leaped out of my chair and ran out the door, leaving it open behind me.

Suddenly the dam holding back my emotions broke, and I couldn't stop crying.

When I got to the corner, other parents told me the bus had broken down a few blocks away and the kids were walking home from there. I ran back home and told Bev and Emma to jump in the car. We drove until we found Lucy on a sidewalk; I rolled down the window and told her to get in. "We're going out to dinner right now," I told her as she tossed her backpack in the back, "and I want to know if you and Emma have been sending me all these white boxes!" At first she passionately denied any involvement, but after I told her that Emma had cracked a little, she broke down and admitted the whole thing. And suddenly the dam holding back my emotions broke, and I couldn't stop crying. We got to the restaurant and I cried all the way through dinner. I cried on the ride home, and I cried myself to sleep. I heard how they pulled off this incredible feat—how they'd found the *Phineas and Ferb* characters at the Disney Store, and how they'd carefully typed and copied the address labels and taped them to the boxes. How they'd planned the exact day and time to leave the boxes in the mailbox. How they'd found the encouraging Scripture passages and laminated them by securing them between two pieces of packing tape. And how Emma, who never, ever kept a secret for more than five minutes, had managed to contain the Godzilla of all secrets for almost two months.

Good news may not lift you when you're really struggling—what really matters is the *giver* of that good news.

Their messages of encouragement, profound and heartfelt as they were, never got past my defenses. But the *messengers* did. My tears that night were in response to the givers of the gift, not the gift itself. The truth about the *Phineas and Ferb* bandits had shocked and undone me because of who was behind it, not because of their encouraging words. Good news may not lift you when you're really struggling—what really matters is the *giver* of that good news.

The great 20th-century media philosopher Marshall McLuhan famously proclaimed: "The medium is the message."[3] A "medium" is an object, device, or person that serves as the conduit for the message. What McLuhan means is that a medium itself, not the content it carries, is the true source of transformational power. To use my earlier illustration, it's more life-transforming to build a relationship with Oprah than to use her recipes. A medium, says McLuhan, influences society not merely by the content it delivers, but by its characteristics. The truth of this dynamic is on display all around us—the medium of texting has fundamentally changed how we communicate with each other, more than the messages we deliver using that medium. In the 20th century, the medium of television replaced the medium of radio, and the new visual technology literally changed our brain chemistry.

The message Jesus brings us is full of hope and promise and redemption. But the *medium* that delivers that message is what gets past our defenses.

And with Jesus, the medium is truly the message. The message Jesus brings us is full of hope and promise and redemption. But the *medium* that delivers that message is what gets past our defenses. When we get to know the heart and passion and personality of WHO is bringing this gospel message—this good news—then the WHO overshadows the WHAT. I couldn't stop crying the night my daughters revealed what they had done, because the medium of the message broke open my closed and battered heart. And when the door of my heart cracked open, Jesus walked through it and healed me. In Eugene Peterson's paraphrase of John 1:14, he writes: "The Word became flesh and blood, and moved into the neighborhood" (The Message). Through the medium of my daughters, the light moved into my darkened neighborhood and rescued me from despair.

Jesus isn't asking us to pick apart his message and catalog our disagreements and struggles with it; he's inviting us to savor what he says and does so well that we end up dining on him. Jesus is the medium for the greatest news we've ever heard, and he himself is the only thing that could ever overshadow that news. If you're a disoriented sheep, caught in the tangle of your own darkness with predators beginning to circle you, you need more than messages of encouragement. You need the Good Shepherd himself to come rescue you—to offer refuge. He is the medium that fuels every freedom-from-captivity message. And when we open the doors of our heart to the Medium of the Message, we discover that we still have doubts and questions and struggles, but we no longer distrust the heart of the Shepherd. We have all the normal responses to life's ups and downs, but we're convinced that Jesus loves us so much that, every day, he lays across the sheepgate on our behalf. We know what a mess we really are—we have no trouble recognizing the sheep in our soul—but we also know "Yes, Jesus loves me...."

And that means we're willing to give ourselves to him like we've never done before.

Endnotes

1 From *The Amazing Race* episode "Get Your Sheep Together," Season 25, Episode 3 (2014).

2 Edwin Friedman, *A Failure of Nerve: Leadership in the Age of the Quick Fix* (New York: Church Publishing, 2007).

3 Marshall McLuhan, *Understanding Media: The Extensions of Man* (New York, NY: McGraw-Hill, 1964).

5

Living a Pig's Life

"God cannot give us a peace apart from Himself. Because there is no other peace."

—C.S. Lewis

At The French Laundry in Napa Valley, the staff won't know what to do if you drop off your unmentionables—it's a laundry in name only. For years it's been one of the world's top-rated restaurants, serving nine-course French-American meals to jacket-required crowds. And if you're a waiter or a dishwasher or a shift manager or a sous chef at The French Laundry, the highest honor you can earn is, well, *a T-shirt*. But not just any T-shirt—this one has a simple slogan stamped on the front: "Be the Pig." To earn that shirt, you'll have to exceed the owners' already stratospheric customer-service standards. The slogan refers to the difference between pigs and chickens: *a chicken might offer up an egg for the meal, but the pig gives his life for it.*

The slogan refers to the difference between pigs and chickens: *a chicken might offer up an egg for the meal, but the pig gives his life for it.*

And people who give themselves to Jesus with a trusting abandon are like pigs. They offer themselves up to him without reservation, because they can't help themselves. Chickens, on the other hand, are more like the tragic early-church couple Ananias and Sapphira—they told the apostles they were gifting the entire purchase price for a piece of property they'd sold, but secretly held back a portion for themselves. They dropped dead when their chicken-y deception was discovered. "And great fear came upon the whole church, and upon all who heard of these things" (Acts 5:11). No doubt. Offering God some but passing it off as all is the sort of thing a chicken does, but it rarely carries a death sentence. The world would be severely underpopulated if that were the case.

Pig-people are ruined by Jesus, and ruined for him.

Pig-people are ruined by Jesus, and ruined for him. And that interior reality enables them to give him their whole heart as a natural response to the beauty that captures them. Talk to people you might consider to be spiritual giants or even saints, and you'll discover they're surprised to be considered this way, and even more surprised that you've assumed their level of spiritual discipline far exceeds your own. Their spiritual practice is really just the expected behavior of those who can't stop thinking about Jesus—they are so grateful to him that service to others is a natural outcome. When you are captured by the beauty of Jesus, you forget to hold back. My girls are both teenagers, so they HATE it when they see my wife and I kiss. But sometimes I'm so captured by her beauty that I kiss her anyway (deal with it, kids). I'm not *working up* my response to her beauty—it's more accurate to say that it *bubbles over*.

This "bubbling over" reality is the fuel behind the overtly extreme language ruined-for-Jesus people often use—extreme language is the vernacular of lovers caught up in a passion they can't appropriately contain. A case in point from C.H. Spurgeon: "If Christ is not all to you He is nothing to you. He will never go into partnership as a part Savior of men. If He be something He must be everything, and if He be not everything He is nothing to you."[1]

"Where Else Would We Go?"

So, what does it mean to be the "pig" in our relationship with Jesus? The clearest biblical translation is an encounter between Jesus and a crowd of thousands, recorded in John 6. It's 2,000 years ago on a lonely Capernaum beachfront. A massive gathering of fanatics has shown up to hear the rock-star Jesus—they're captivated by his miracles, healings, and teachings. And on this day Jesus tells them something that, at first, seems confusing—but then it dawns on them that he must be insane. Jesus tells them, *nine times in a row*, to eat the flesh of the Son of Man and drink his blood or have "no life in yourselves." They ask for clarification, but Jesus simply repeats himself, over and over. And they're quickly disgusted and disoriented enough to escape him en masse.

Thousands of boisterous Mediterranean people retreating in a massive, noisy rush? That likely sounded like an elephant stampede, with all those sandaled feet kicking up a towering dust cloud. And after the chaos and noise from their retreat has died down, Jesus looks at his core 12 disciples—also likely disgusted and disoriented by his inscrutable proclamation—and asks this incredible question: "You do not want to go away also, do you?" It's maybe the most vulnerable question ever asked, because it's God asking it. And, here, Peter steps to the plate and answers like a pig, so to speak:

"Lord, to whom shall we go? You have words of eternal life. We believe and know that you are the Holy One of God."

Peter, like the masses who've just stampeded from Capernaum, scrambling to get away from the half-insane Jesus, would likely escape him if he could. But he just can't. He likely doesn't understand what Jesus has just said any better than the angry crowd that has rejected him. But Peter so identifies himself with Jesus that he can't imagine leaving him. Peter is all-in—*a pig, not a chicken*—and this is exactly the kind of relationship Jesus is longing for. When we so identify ourselves with Jesus that we can't imagine leaving him, then we're pigs. Even more, when we are captured by the gravitational pull of his black-hole presence in our lives, we can't scramble our way back across the event horizon. We're hurtling into the center of the heart of Jesus, no matter where it takes us...

Remember that Paul, one of the great pigs of all time—also one of the greatest thinkers and certainly the greatest apologist in history—describes his orientation to Jesus this way: "I determined to know nothing among you except Jesus Christ, and Him crucified" (1 Corinthians 2:2). What does he mean by "know nothing"? He is, of course, using hyperbole to emphasize his passion—to spend his energy and his intellect and his emotional capabilities to know Jesus with pig-like determination. He's not interested in facts and trivia and right answers about Jesus. Paul wants to know him the way you know your best friends or, even more accurately, your lover—inside-out. Paul wants to know him so well that he can finish his sentences. That's living a pig's life.

But most of us have bought into a flawed strategy for spiritual maturity that produces chicken-caution, not pig-abandonment. I call it the "understand and apply" strategy—it's the preferred spiritual growth imperative of most evangelical churches in the Western world, and the go-to sermon outline for most pastors. It assumes people grow deeper in their faith when they understand biblical principles and apply them to their lives. But "understand and apply" has proven to be a marginal strategy, at best, and has weak biblical support. Jesus did not use it as his primary teaching strategy—he preferred debriefed experiences, conversations, surprising questions, and narrative metaphors. When I've asked people how they've been transformed by their relationship with Jesus, none have cited a biblical truth they applied to their lives.

The ultimate reason so many of us follow Jesus half-heartedly, or no-heartedly, is that *we can.*

The ultimate reason so many of us follow Jesus half-heartedly, or no-heartedly, is that *we can.* I mean, we're not ruined for him, as Peter was when Jesus asked if he was going to leave, too. A disciple's answer to that question is something like: "I don't understand a lot of what you're saying, and I can't comprehend the things you do, but I know I have nowhere else to go. You've ruined me for you." Disciples answer this way because of the depth of their attachment to Jesus. And they've become deeply attached because they have simply decided to get to know him as he really is, not as they've been told he is. Because of the vast number of lesser gods that are demanding our attention, *only* a deeper attachment to Jesus has any chance of stopping our slide toward the abyss of our mid-marriage malaise with God.

Application vs. Attachment

To help us understand what he's aiming for in his relationship with us, Jesus uses a botanical metaphor: "I am the Vine, you are the branches. When you're joined with me and I with you, the relation intimate and organic, the harvest is sure to be abundant. Separated, you can't produce a thing. Anyone who separates from me is deadwood, gathered up and thrown on the bonfire" (John 15:5-6, The Message). This joined-to-the-Vine metaphor is telling us a deep truth: We are dying branches in desperate need of attaching ourselves to a growing Vine, and the Vine is Jesus himself. Later, Paul builds on the foundation of Jesus' metaphor by extending its meaning: "If some of the branches have been broken off, and you, though a wild olive shoot, have been grafted in among the others and now share in the nourishing sap from the olive root, do not consider yourself to be superior to those other branches. If you do, consider this: You do not support the root, but the root supports you" (Romans 11:17-18, NIV).

Transformation happens when we attach ourselves more deeply to Jesus, because he's the only one who can really change us. Transformation comes when we have the life of the Vine flowing in us, not when we've mastered a long list of spiritual disciplines. A self that is fully alive and fully itself is the organic outcome of a deepening attachment to the Vine. And it's the organic outcome that Jesus is after, not understanding and applying—which sounds Christian-y and positive, but is not the gospel of Jesus Christ. The understand-and-apply formula for maturity and transformation rests on two commonly accepted fallacies...

1. **Understand-and-apply assumes that mere understanding leads to growth.** If understanding was a true indicator of growth as a disciple, then Satan should step to the head of the class. He knew enough biblical truth to go toe-to-toe with Jesus in the wilderness. Understanding alone does not guarantee transformation. The Enlightenment kicked off a common understanding about rational

thought that is now a given in our culture: The most important ingredient in any recipe for growth or maturation is the progression of thought. On one level, that would mean the smartest people are also the most mature, and it takes very little investigative effort to debunk that premise. In fact, you'd be hard-pressed to make the case that Jesus' disciples upended the ancient world because of their advanced understanding of biblical truth. No, they upended the ancient world because they'd been transformed by their intimate relationship with the Spirit of Jesus, now living inside them because of Pentecost.

"That's right," we say, "because we must also apply our understanding to our life—that's what the disciples did, and Satan never has done. It's the application of our understanding that produces transformation." That brings us to fallacy #2...

2. **Understand-and-apply assumes our growth in Christ is dependent on our ability, or willingness, to apply truth to our lives.** Anything that is founded upon the strength of our efforts is flawed and inherently limiting. Try this experiment the next time you're listening to a sermon or reading a Christian living book: Count the number of times some version of "apply this to your life" is mentioned. Then ask yourself: *What's the likelihood that I'll immediately begin applying these truths to my life?* Or even more telling: *What's the likelihood that I even* understand *how to apply the truths I've just heard, or have the willpower to consider applying them?* Another way of assessing your adherence to this standard is this simple test: *What apply-it-to-my-life imperative did I pick up from the last time I was in church, and how did I end up living it out in my life?* We feel guilty about our grade in the apply-it-to-life category because we're living under an impossible prerequisite for growth and transformation.

If we added up all the applications we hear on a yearly basis, we'd have a big number—much bigger than our own relatively tiny capacity for catalyzing transformation can handle. "Apply this to your life" is the most over-used, under-scrutinized given in the Christian life. In our Stockdale

Paradox approach, we have to confront the brutal realities surrounding this sacred cow: *We're not very good at applying things to our life, and even when we're successful at it, transformation into a more Christ-like version of our character is sketchy at best.* Remember, some of the best practitioners of the apply-it-to-life mantra were also some of the worst examples of spiritual maturity—the Pharisees that Jesus lambasted over and over.

If we added up all the applications we hear on a yearly basis, we'd have a big number—much bigger than our own relatively tiny capacity for catalyzing transformation can handle.

The Pharisees and teachers of the law preferred the scorekeeping efficiency of understand-and-apply over the messiness of sloppy wet kisses. No one understood God's law better, and no one spent more time and energy thinking through how to apply those laws into every conceivable situation—they made a cottage industry out of it. "Once, on being asked by the Pharisees when the kingdom of God would come, Jesus replied, 'The kingdom of God is not something that can be observed, nor will people say, "Here it is," or "There it is," because the kingdom of God is in your midst' " (Luke 17:20-21, NIV). We do not enter into the kingdom of God by careful observation of God's principles—the kingdom is not something outside of us that we apply to our lives. It is the lifeblood of the Vine, and only the grafted-in branches share in it. Jesus assesses the Pharisees' application mentality this way: "Woe to you! For you are like concealed tombs, and the people who walk over them are unaware of it" (Luke 11:44).

Jesus' own template for spiritual growth is nothing like this understand-and-apply strategy. He invites us to attach ourselves to him, grafting us into his essence—our identity is then hidden in him, and fruit results. Paul explains it this way: "Therefore, my brethren, you also were made to die to the Law through the body of Christ, that you might be joined to another, to Him who was raised from the dead, that we might bear fruit for God" (Romans 7:4). And again, writing to the church in Colossae, he says: "Set your mind on the things above, not on the things that are on earth. For you have died and your life is hidden with Christ in God. When Christ, who is our life, is revealed, then you also will be revealed with Him in glory" (Colossians 3:2-4).

Transformation is the natural result of grafting in the organic world. Botanists tell us that the bond between the grafted branch and the vine transforms the branch into a miniature version of the parent tree.[2] This is why, by the way, Jesus can make this ludicrous statement with a straight face: "Truly, truly, I say to you, he who believes in Me, the works that I do he will do also; and greater works than these he will do; because I go to the Father" (John 14:12). If our attachment to him essentially makes us a miniature version of the parent tree, the fruit we produce will be like his own, and even greater.

Our grafted bond is intimate but not instantaneous—it takes a long time for it to take. Our transformations, whether they're physical or spiritual, are often so slow-moving that we have a hard time noticing the profound changes that are happening in the moment. They are most often like a glacier—an inexorable force that changes our geography, though it's hard to mark progress at any particular time. Transformation is most often a time-lapse thing. But the deeper our attachment to Jesus, the more he transforms us, making us whole again, as Adam and Eve were in the Garden of Eden before the Fall.

"How are you going to know the truth of your being unless somebody tells you what the truth of your being is?"

I asked a wise writer friend, a man who seems at rest with himself, what wholeness really means. Here's what he said: "Wholeness is when the way of your being matches the truth of your being. That begs the question, what's the truth of your being? This is where this understanding of Jesus at the center of all the cosmos becomes absolutely critical. How are you going to know the truth of your being unless somebody tells you what the truth of your being is?" The other truth about our being is that we are wired by God to thrive as pigs—the chicken life is contrary to our core identity.

Because we are created in his image, we are living whole when we are giving ourselves in trusting abandon to him.

Rejecting Circumstantial Security

If you're more like a chicken than a pig in the way you live out your relationship with God (and who isn't, at least some of the time?), then Jesus is always on trial in your life. I mean, if things are going well, then Jesus is good. But if things are not going well—and especially if they're calamitous—then doubt sets in about God's goodness and reliability. And that makes sense, because the two-stroke question at the core of every human being is simple: Is God real, and is God good? And, we have to admit, our experiences in life bully us into chicken-like responses. We hedge our bets and compartmentalize our relationship with Jesus, or we gravitate to lesser gods, all because we crave circumstantial security. Our assessment of God's heart condenses down to how often, and how well, he comes through for us. Of course, all of us want good things to happen in our lives, and we're desperate to be rescued from bad things. When the Apostle Paul says, "I have learned the secret of living in every situation, whether it is with a full stomach or empty, with plenty or little" (Philippians 4:11-12), we want to scream, "Good for you, Paul, but I'm not a spiritual giant like you!"

God longs for a pig-like romance, not a chicken-like transaction.

This if/then cadence about the goodness of God in our lives exposes the default setting in our relationship with him—we have embraced a transactional approach that gives only when it gets. The American Dream is a good example of transactional living. At its heart is the widely embraced myth that if we work hard and maintain a basic level of goodness, we'll earn a guarantee from the cosmos that ensures a reasonably comfortable life—in Western culture that most often translates to a house, two cars, two kids, a vacation or two every year, and a comfortable retirement. It's hard for us to think outside of this prevailing success narrative because it promises us the certainty that we will get something if we give something.

Three-quarters of Americans say the American Dream is still possible and achievable.[3] This transactional way of seeing life extends to every area of our lives, including our relationship with God. If we're honest, it's difficult for most of us to assess that relationship outside of a "I give him something, then he gives me something" expectation. We hold to an unspoken and often unconscious standard: *What will following Jesus do for me?* But God longs for a pig-like romance, not a chicken-like transaction. David Nasser says: "The highest reward of the gospel is not that we get forgiveness, but that we get God."[4] So true, but often not visceral enough to supplant our transactional get-when-I-give default setting.

Here's what I mean…

Not long ago, on my way home from work, the clutch in my 1995 Volvo failed in the middle of rush-hour traffic on a busy highway. Then my phone died while I was on hold for AAA service. My broken-down car was blocking the left lane, creating a swell of angry drivers who glared at me as they maneuvered past.

Is God good?

A policeman showed up and offered to shove me out of traffic. He pushed me to the top of a hill so I could coast down the other side to a wide shoulder off the highway. Then I borrowed his phone, called my wife, and waited two hours for the tow truck to show up.

Is God good?

When the driver finally arrived, he told me his truck was on empty and he'd need to get some gas right away. He needed diesel—late at night in an unfamiliar part of town. Three failed attempts later, he found an open station that had diesel and we finally got back on the highway. An hour later, I dragged my tired carcass through the door of my darkened home.

Is God good?

The next day, the mechanic at the place where we towed the car called to tell me he'd found the problem. The fix was expensive, but not too expensive.

Is God good?

Meanwhile, that very morning, it looked like my wife's crazy-impossible idea for taking our daughter Lucy on a surprise 16th-birthday trip to New

York City might actually happen. A friend of a friend had offered us her Upper West Side walk-up as a free place to stay, and that morning the cost of the flights had suddenly dropped dramatically. We knew they could go up again at any time. "We have to do this now if we're going to do this," I told my wife. So I clicked on "Book" and exhaled...

Is God good?

Two hours after I bit my lip and bought those tickets, the mechanic called. Once he had the car up on the rack, he found bigger problems. The cost of the fix had gone way, way up—probably twice what the car was actually worth. I knew in that moment, the old grey horse was dead. And now, after pulling the trigger on a financially extravagant trip that we didn't need, we faced the financial necessity of finding and paying for a replacement car.

Is God good?

Or, more specifically, is he the God who managed to pull all the right strings and make it possible for us to surprise our daughter with a celebratory trip she'd never forget, or is he the God who sat on his hands while our car breathed its last?

Is God good and trustworthy, or is God capricious and untrustworthy?

Everything in life—everything—rests on whether or not God is good. We will never be able to figure him out, in the moment, by studying the shifting fortunes of our circumstances. And if we're asking, as I often do, "Is God good?" after each nasty/joyful twist in our road, we'll find ourselves with a chicken's faith in Jesus. No, the time to decide whether or not God is good is *not* in the thick of our circumstances. That's circumstantial security. It's the sheep distrusting the Shepherd because the sheep happened to get caught in the brambles as it was wandering through the underbrush.

Everything in life—everything—rests on whether or not God is good.

If Jesus came to show us exactly who God is, then we'll only understand and trust the heart of God if we understand and trust the heart of Jesus. And when you slow down to pursue the heart of Jesus—to taste and see it—you'll discover something staggeringly good. His heart is more good than our churched, Sunday school, Bible-study-group descriptions have typically led us to believe. He's good at a level so deep that he shatters every other definition of good. As Peter Kreeft says, Jesus' beauty is shocking. Jesus is not only the Way, the Truth, and the Life; he is also the Good.

And when we're in the middle of a dark place, what we want is our circumstances to change from darkness to light—we are all chicken-hearted in the heat of the moment. But the difference a pig-disciple brings to the table is simple: If you are ruined for Jesus, then your verdict on his goodness was decided *way before* your calamity, and your assessment is irreversible. Chickens go halfway because they're weighing their takeaway in the relationship. Their transactional relationship with Jesus is boundaried by give-and-take: "If you give me what I want, then I'll give you what you want: my allegiance." But pigs say: "If you give me nothing of what I want, and I still have you, then I'm good." They say this not because they're spiritual giants, but because they've been captured by the heart of Jesus— not by what's inside his treasure box. Failure and calamity still hurt, maybe even more so, because our hearts are more tender and less guarded than ever before. But we are surprised when our core reaction is akin to Paul's: "For I consider that the sufferings of this present time are not worthy to be compared with the glory that is to be revealed to us" (Romans 8:18).

The brutal reality is that some failures are like the bottom of a porta-potty.

We're told that failure is our best teacher. Well, the success-from-failure equation is no doubt often true, but the brutal reality is that some failures are like the bottom of a porta-potty. These are the sorts of failures that cover us with a stink we're not sure we can ever scrub off. A couple of summers ago I led the program for our church's family camp. As the speaker, my job was to plan three gatherings that would capture, engage, and challenge an impossible range of ages—from toddlers to grandparents. I take lots of risks in what I do, so I never know for sure what will work and what won't. Well, the first two nights went really well—late Saturday night my daughter Lucy looked at me with tears in her eyes and said, "Sometimes I can't believe you're actually my dad." That's a "wow" moment for any dad. But when Sunday morning was a semi-disaster, that same daughter stopped me and said, "Dad, how could you blow it so badly?"

Failure is like that Russian Greco-Roman wrestler Alexander Karelin—you can circle him on the mat, but he will pin you sooner or later.

It's possible, I've discovered, to live in the porta-potty of failure without finding the trap door that leads to the fresh air of redemptive success.

We rightly fear failure like we fear any other threat to life and limb. The reason we watch horror movies is because they haul our nightmares out from behind the curtain of our future and let us poke at them a little. We tame the thing we fear most by inoculating ourselves with a little bit of it. And we try to declaw failure by telling ourselves that it's the necessary prerequisite for success, and that we must embrace it before we can get past it. But if a pig-disciple says, "Even if I taste failure and heartbreak and disaster, if I still have you I will have everything I need," then there's no need to recontextualize failure or spray a little perfume on it. It's possible, I've discovered, to live in the porta-potty of failure without finding the trap door that leads to the fresh air of redemptive success.

When you let your eyes adjust to the dark confines of that porta-potty, you discover there's a guy down there leaning against a wall, as if he's waiting for you. "Hey," he says, "you're here." And you squint and ask, "Who are you?" And you see the faint outline of his hand extended to you as he says, "It's Jesus. I live here." And your eyes get big and you ask, with obvious shock, "You live here?" And he says, "Yep. I've been waiting for you. Now that you're here, maybe we can hang out. Got the time?" And you say, "As it turns out, yes I do."

In his theological masterwork *The Gospel in a Pluralistic Society*, author and missionary Lesslie Newbigin describes what he calls the "piercing paradox" of Jesus this way: "[We] ought to direct our minds away from our programs to the awesome reality of God whose sovereignty is manifest in what the world calls failure."[5]

The Smell of Jesus

Scripture tells us that Jesus does have a smell, and it's not a porta-potty smell. Or is it? His smell would most likely remind *you* of fresh-baked bread, but to others it smells more like that latrine he lives in. "For we are a fragrance of Christ to God among those who are being saved and among those who are perishing; to the one an aroma from death to death, to the other an aroma from life to life" (2 Corinthians 2:15-16). The fragrance of Christ—life to life—is a scent we want to wallow in. And the closer we get to him, the more his smell rubs off on us.

The fragrance of Christ—life to life—is a scent we want to wallow in.

We don't want mere data about Jesus—we want to experience him often enough and truly enough that his smell rubs off on us. Let's revisit Jesus' encounter with the woman at the well in John 4. After she mistakes what he's offering her (she thinks he intends to draw water from the well for her), Jesus tells her the water from Jacob's Well is nothing compared to the living water of himself. He wants her to drink of him—an invitation to know him so intimately that her thirst (longing for something more in life) would be quenched forever. Put another way, he wants his smell to rub off on her. When I was engaged to my wife, I used one of her old T-shirts as a pillowcase, just because I loved her smell and wanted to be reminded of it. And the Bible is a lot like my wife's old T-shirt—we return to it, over and over, to remind ourselves of the smell of Jesus.

John, nicknamed "the disciple whom Jesus loved," records a stunning scene on the shores of the Sea of Tiberias (John 21). Here, after the resurrection of Jesus, a restless Peter tells the other disciples that he's going fishing; six of them join him, fishing all night and catching nothing. At daybreak they see a man on the shore, calling to them: "Children, you do not have any fish, do you?" Nope. So the man tells them to cast their net on the right side of the boat—"and then they were not able to haul it in because of the great number of fish." As they are fighting to bring the catch into the boat,

John points to the shore and says: "It is the Lord!" And Peter scrunches up his eyes to confirm that it's Jesus, and then explodes with desire…

He's stripped naked for work, because that's how fisherman did it back in the day. But he must get to Jesus NOW. So he quickly ties his garment around his waist and, like a child rushing to meet his soldier daddy who's home from the war, plunges into the choppy waters and swims furiously to shore. The boat follows behind as Peter thrashes his way to Jesus, who is calmly building a fire so they can have breakfast together. When Peter arrives, panting and naked and dripping wet, he stands before Jesus. In the Garden, Adam and Eve stood before God "naked and unashamed." Now Peter stands again before God, naked and unashamed. Maybe he's the first person since the Fall of humankind to do it.

When we are pigs, and we are covered in the smell of Jesus because we've given ourselves to him with abandon, the self-consciousness that sin and betrayal creates in us is obliterated. Our passion for Jesus overshadows our fear of embarrassment. We stand naked and unafraid in his presence.

What kinds of people change the world? Well, we assume it's the really smart ones—the highly talented, most widely connected, best-educated, and most-driven people have what it takes. So how do we explain the ragtag group of nobodies Jesus chose as his closest disciples and confidants—the mostly uneducated blue-collar grunts who ended up changing the world so profoundly that everyone everywhere is affected by what they did? The simple reason these often clueless first-century men and women upended the world is because their movement was attached to the present force of the person of Jesus. They weren't the greatest tips-and-techniques people who ever walked the earth. They weren't skilled at strategy or structure. But they were ruined for Jesus, and that reality changed everything they touched.

Real impact in the world isn't ultimately tied to our gifts and abilities; it's tied to *his* gifts and abilities empowering us to move mountains because we are intimately attached to him.

In his book *Who Is This Man?* author and pastor John Ortberg sums it up well: "Normally when someone dies, their impact on the world immediately begins to recede. But… Jesus' impact was greater a hundred years after His death than during his life; it was greater still after five hundred years; after a thousand years His legacy laid the foundation for much of Europe; after two thousand years He has more followers in more places than ever."[6] Real impact in the world isn't ultimately tied to our gifts and abilities; it's tied to *his* gifts and abilities empowering us to move mountains because we are intimately attached to him.

Jesus, in the Garden of Gethsemane, prays: "Father, if you are willing, please take this cup of suffering away from me. Yet I want your will to be done, not mine" (Luke 22:42, NLT). His two-sentence prayer sums up the Stockdale Paradox rhythm in a pig's heart: *I see the brutal reality, and I want to be rescued from it, but there is no part of me that isn't yours, so I give myself to your will.* This submission to the heart of God is not a religious imperative; it's a determination to live in a prevailing hope that is guaranteed by his goodness. Because the heart of Jesus is exactly like the heart of the God we can't see, and our own hearts are fashioned after his, we are living in congruence with our redeemed identity when we live like pigs. You can feel it when you chew on Jesus' prayer—your heart knows what he is doing is heroic and good, because your heart and his heart speak the same language.

Of course, we can "pig out" on many other somethings besides God— but they do not have the strength, purity, love, and determination to receive the weight of our lives when we offer it. We all know that squirmy feeling that comes when we see someone giving their whole life to an inconsequential pursuit—we admire 16-year-old girls who've given up their childhood to pursue their Olympic dreams, but we'd never make the same sacrifice ourselves. If we give the whole of ourselves to Jesus, he will know what to do with us. That's a statement of trust, and there's nothing blind about it, as long as we've already answered the most important question in our journey…

Endnotes

1 Charles Haddon Spurgeon, "Christ Is All," Volume 61, Sermon #3446—Colossians 3:11.

2 Taken from the YouTube video "Grafting Fruit Trees," produced by Daley's Fruit Tree Nursery in Kyogle, Australia.

3 From a 2011 poll by Allstate and the *National Journal*.

4 From David Nasser's biography on The Gospel Coalition web site—thegospelcoalition.org.

5 Lesslie Newbigin, *The Gospel in a Pluralist Society* (Grand Rapids, MI: Eerdmans, 1989), 224.

6 John Ortberg, *Who Is This Man?* (Grand Rapids, MI: Zondervan, 2012), 11-12.

The First-and-Only Question
That Really Matters

"A man who was merely a man and said the sort of things Jesus said would not be a great moral teacher. He would either be a lunatic—on the level with the man who says he is a poached egg—or else he would be the Devil of Hell. You must make your choice. Either this man was, and is, the Son of God, or else a madman or something worse. You can shut him up for a fool, you can spit at him and kill him as a demon or you can fall at his feet and call him Lord and God, but let us not come with any patronizing nonsense about his being a great human teacher. He has not left that open to us. He did not intend to."

—C.S. Lewis

Jesus and his disciples are road-tripping through Caesarea Philippi, stopping to heal the lame, crippled, blind, and dumb and to feed a crowd of thousands with seven loaves of bread and a few small fish—just another average day in the Messiah's traveling Cirque du Soleil. But then, after the latest in a long line of tough encounters with the conniving Pharisees, followed by another frustrating conversation with his well-meaning but often-clueless disciples, Jesus does something shockingly humble. He asks his best friends a courageous question: "Who do people say that the Son of Man is?"

His nervous disciples shuffle their sandals, cast sideways glances at each other, then offer this: "Some say John the Baptist; and others, Elijah; but still others, Jeremiah, or one of the prophets."

And here is Jesus at his most vulnerable: *"But who do you say that I am?"*

When is the last time you asked your friends, "What do you think of me, really?" This moment is awkward, to say the least, saturated in self-consciousness and unspoken expectations. The disciples are staring at their toes and waiting for someone to break the tension. And, of course, a determined Simon throws this high-stakes answer on the table: *"You are the Christ, the Son of the living God."*

Here is why Simon Peter is such a heroic figure in the Bible—he steps up in yet another epic and awkward moment and proclaims the truth about who Jesus really is. It is an astonishing answer, and one that will eventually lead to Peter's martyrdom, crucified upside-down on a cross. But the electricity produced by his answer is overshadowed by the question that invited it: "Who do you say I am?" This is a question for the ages—for you and me, not just for a dozen men on a dusty journey through the Golan Heights.

The first-and-only question that really matters in life is this: *Who do I say Jesus is?*

It's not an answer-once question—it's an answer-now and now-again question. And the way we describe and understand Jesus will define our present, reframe our past, and guide our future. The pinpoint focus of "Who do I say Jesus is?" both simplifies and expands our purpose in life—when a driving curiosity propels our fascination with everything he says and does, we grow more and more sensitive to his Spirit's nudges and instruction. When we answer, over and over, "Who do you say I am?" we move Jesus from the periphery to the center of our lives. He's no longer playing the role of divine butler—a useful servant who comes when we call and retreats to his quarters when he's not needed.

Notre Dame professor of sociology Dr. Christian Smith led the most ambitious research project targeting faith beliefs and practices in the U.S. that's ever been attempted. Smith is the one who came up with the divine butler description for Jesus, based on how more than 3,000 adolescents and their parents described their relationship with him. Smith says most Americans, adults and kids alike, live a "wallpaper" life with God: "[People had] extreme difficulty in explaining how [their religious practice] affected their lives, other than to say it makes them happy, helps them have a better day, and helps them make some good moral decisions. It seems like religion operates in the background—it's just part of the wallpaper, part of the furniture."[1]

"Who do I say Jesus is?" is the *central question* for those who would be his disciples.

Religion, as archaic and formulaic as it sounds to us, is simply the language we use to describe how we relate to God. So if Jesus, and the way we relate to him, is merely part of the furniture of our life, then we are never drinking from the life-replenishing stream of his mission and purpose. That's why "Who do I say Jesus is?" is the *central question* for those who would be his disciples. All other questions fit under its expanse. It's our guide into a life of great purpose, eternal significance, and thirsty intimacy. In contrast, when we assume we know everything there is to know about Jesus, boredom is the natural outcome. That's when we move into Jesus-plus mode.

When we're "been there, done that" with him, we turn our attention to the tips-and-techniques that will make our life work better. For many of us, our soul is not satisfied by a sorta/kinda focus on him—it's simply not enough for us. The diagnostic markers for this restless relationship with the Jesus-plus life include disappointment, disillusionment, and an insatiable need to buy or experience the next big thing. But instead of taking a deeper bite into the apple who is Jesus, to get to his core, it's easy enough to turn our attention to the bowl of plastic fruit offered to us as a safer alternative to his body and blood. Our God-plus life is a pragmatic attempt to replace one great love with a lot of lesser (and ultimately unsatisfying) loves, to help us hang in there in life. And soon, the Jesus we think we know bears little resemblance to the Jesus that Peter is describing.

Out of the Mouths of Babes

A few years ago I was in Canada, leading a mix of adult and teenage ministry leaders from a very conservative denomination through my "Jesus-Centered" experience. In one section of the experience, small teams wrestle with a series of Scripture passages that are intended to introduce them to the Jesus they never knew. At the end of this process I ask groups to finish this statement: "Jesus is..." They can finish it any way they want, based on their exploration of Jesus through Scripture. As group after group called out their "Jesus is" statements, I wrote them on a huge flipchart at the front of the room. It has always been a profound and surprising and even life-changing experience for many. On this day, I was about halfway through my survey of the room when I got to a table full of teenage girls. I pointed to the table and one of them, the designated speaker, stood up and proclaimed, in a very loud voice: *"Jesus is a badass!"*

Then she sat down.

What followed was a *very* pregnant pause—a moment that splashed me with terror as I waited for this eclectic group of buttoned-up ministry people to react to the girl's raw proclamation. And then, like a concussion bomb, the room erupted in delighted glee. The clapping and laughter spiraled together and rolled through the room like a tsunami. And I couldn't stop smiling as this straight-laced gathering of ministry people persisted in applauding the teenager's declaration—her description of Jesus had captured and channeled the pent-up passion of the moment. And, maybe like me, they knew "badass" was as close to a dead-on portrait of the heart of Jesus as we were likely to hear in our lifetime. When the ruckus finally died down I told the girl that I'd never given a prize for an answer in any of my training experiences—ever—but she had just forced me into an exception.

I think any fair reading of the Gospels, with preconceived assumptions muted, would result in a similar "Jesus is..." statement for anyone who has the courage (or the adolescent chutzpah) to say it. In the vernacular of a teenage girl who doesn't know any better, *he's a redemptive badass, and our freedom from captivity is possible because of it.* If Satan, the enemy of God, is committed to persevere in his killing, stealing, and destroying, then our Redeemer, the Shepherd who intends to lay down his life for his sheep, had better be up for the fight. And, it turns out, the outcome of this confrontation underscores Jesus' blunt declaration: "Do not fear those who kill the body but are unable to kill the soul; but rather fear Him who is able to destroy both soul and body in hell" (Matthew 10:28).

We've been led to believe that we should fear Satan because he's just like the "baddest man in town" described in Jim Croce's iconic song "Bad, Bad Leroy Brown"—he's "badder than old King Kong, and meaner than a junkyard dog." But in the song, when baddest Leroy starts messing with another man's wife, and that man takes exception to Mr. Brown, he discovers that the man he underestimated puts up a fight that's way more than he bargained for: "And when they pulled them from the floor, Leroy looked like a jigsaw puzzle with a couple of pieces gone."[2] Now, metaphorically, that's a fair description of what Satan looked like after the crucifixion and resurrection of Jesus. The book of Revelation describes the scene: "Together they will go to war against the Lamb, but the Lamb will defeat them because he is Lord of all lords and King of all kings" (Revelation 17:14, NLT).

Is it okay to answer the question, "Who do I say that Jesus is?" by referencing a lyric from "Bad, Bad Leroy Brown"? Maybe it pushes the envelope too far. But better to push the envelope on the side of fierce or even dangerous-for-good than to allow the predominant description of Jesus—Mr. Rogers in an earth-tone cardigan—to remain an uncontested myth. When "Who do I say that Jesus is?" morphs from a curiosity to a fascination to a passion, our life enters into a promised land that is rich with significance, intimacy, and joy.

Permanent Curiosity

Jesus asks his disciples what the crowds are saying about him, and the answers they relay to him not only miss the target, they miss the hay bale that frames the target. And our own answers to this fundamental question are often, we must admit, closer to what the crowds are saying than to Peter's bold declaration. Like the people of Israel, most of us in contemporary culture are generally comfortable describing Jesus as a good person, a great teacher, and even a catalytic prophet. Some will call him God, but they will mean "alien" when they say it.

Have we so assumed the plausibility of our response to "Who do I say that Jesus is?" that we have stopped asking ourselves the question? Have we already slotted Jesus the way the crowds who flocked to see his miracle sideshow slotted him?

It's human nature to live within the boundaries of plausible beliefs, whether or not they're true. That means we prefer plausible explanations for things even if they are not truthful explanations. A short list of plausible explanations that we've accepted as true, but are not:

• The Great Wall of China is not the only manmade object visible from space, and the wall is actually very difficult to see. The most easily seen object is Alberta's manmade tailing ponds, but that's not as plausibly compelling as China's iconic wall.

• It's not harmful to pick up baby birds and return them to their nests, and their mothers will not reject them because they sense human on them.

• The Bible never identifies the forbidden fruit that Adam and Eve eat as an apple. It was much more likely a fig or a pomegranate.

• Vikings didn't actually wear horns on their helmets—that was an artistic flourish for the costumes in a Wagner opera performed in 1876.

• Life expectancy for people living in the Middle Ages wasn't in the 30s. Infant mortality was high, but if you survived into adulthood you could expect to live into your 60s.

Once we embrace a plausible explanation for something, it's very difficult to let go of it, whether or not it's true, simply because plausibility creates a powerful bullet-proof narrative. Missionary and theologian Lesslie Newbigin says: "Every society depends for its coherence upon a set of what Peter Berger calls 'plausibility structures,' patterns of beliefs and practice accepted within a given society, which determine which beliefs are plausible to its members and which are not. These plausibility structures are of course different at different times and places. Thus when, in any society, a belief is held to be 'reasonable,' this is a judgment made on the basis of the reigning plausibility structure."[3]

A merely nice Jesus fits our plausible belief that life is really about trying harder to be a good person.

The reigning plausibility structure in our culture, relative to Jesus, is that he is more like Mr. Rogers than the guy who made Leroy Brown look like a jigsaw puzzle with pieces missing. A merely nice Jesus fits our plausible belief that life is really about trying harder to be a good person. He has set a standard of niceness for us that is beyond our reach, but nevertheless our aim. Nice Jesus doesn't really ask us for pig-like commitment anyway—he's plausibly content for us to relate with him like chickens. The chicken life, where we offer some but not all of our heart, is what seems attainable under our own power and control. And Nice Jesus wouldn't want us to elevate him over everything else in our life, because that wouldn't be a nice thing for us.

The mission of Jesus is to show us the good heart of God and then to rebuild the trust we need to be intimate with him.

The question is this: Have we so understood our plausible Jesus that our pursuit of him is far less interesting to us than the pursuit of social relationships or postmodern worship or artistic expressions of the Christian life or culturally relevant approaches to Bible study? *"Who do I say that Jesus is?"* is much more than a question to be answered. It's the navigational North Star of our life's pursuit—whatever direction we go in life, we're always heading "north" toward him, no matter if we have to tack to the left or right along the way. We're always pointing in this direction because there is no other way, because he is the Way. We can't have the intimacy with Jesus that he longs for if we're relating to a fake, substitute Jesus. The path into intimacy is through the door of truth. When we experience and embrace, more and more every day, the truth about Jesus, then our hearts naturally open to trust him. For most people, intimacy with *anyone* in their lives can seem out of reach, because their trust has been violated over and over. The mission of Jesus is to show us the good heart of God and then to rebuild the trust we need to be intimate with him.

Paul begins the fifth chapter of his letter to the Roman believers with this:

Therefore, since we have been made right in God's sight by faith, we have peace with God because of what Jesus Christ our Lord has done for us. Because of our faith, Christ has brought us into this place of undeserved privilege where we now stand, and we confidently and joyfully look forward to sharing God's glory. We can rejoice, too, when we run into problems and trials, for we know that they help us develop endurance. And endurance develops strength of character, and character strengthens our confident hope of salvation. And this hope will not lead to disappointment. For we know how dearly God loves us, because he has given us the Holy Spirit to fill our hearts with his love (Romans 5:1-5, NLT).

We will not be disappointed by our hope in God, because Jesus is showing us the heart of God, and the Spirit is giving us an experience of his love. Whatever we do, we must pursue *"Who do I say that Jesus is?"* because the question, even more than the answer, will lead us each to the life our soul has always longed for.

Endnotes

1 Dr. Christian Smith, quoted in the article "Youth Ministry's Impact!" in the May/June 2006 issue of *Group Magazine*.

2 From "Bad, Bad Leroy Brown," written by Jim Croce, lyrics © Sony/ATV Music Publishing LLC.

3 Newbigin, *The Gospel in a Pluralist Society*, 8.

7

The Second-and-Only Question That Really Matters

"[Jesus] lived serenely, as a greater artist than all other artists, despising marble and clay as well as color, working in living flesh. That is to say, this matchless artist...made neither statues nor pictures nor books; he loudly proclaimed that he made...living men, immortals."

—Vincent Van Gogh

When Simon steps up to answer Jesus' question ("Who do you say that I am?") with magnificent determination, he reveals his deepening attachment to Jesus, the Vine. But close relationships are always mutually generous—we consider the truth about who Jesus really is and "name" him, and Jesus considers the truth about who we are and "names" us. Yes, his close friend, the fisherman with the flashing eyes, is the first to publicly proclaim him as Messiah and the Son of God. But then Jesus fires back with this:

You are Peter, and upon this rock I will build My church; and the gates of Hades will not overpower it. I will give you the keys of the kingdom of heaven; and whatever you bind on earth shall have been bound in heaven, and whatever you loose on earth shall have been loosed in heaven (Matthew 16:18-19).

As we have the courage to name Jesus, he is just as determined to name us, as he does with Simon by revealing his true name. "Petros" had never before been used as a name—it literally means "rock," so it would be like naming your newborn "Spandex" or "Lathe." Jesus is the first to give anyone, anywhere the name "Peter." When we narrow our focus on Jesus, pay better attention to him, and even feed on all the surprising things he says and does, we also invite him to identify who we really are and what we're made to do in life. It's what my writer friend is after when he asks: "How are you going to know the truth of your being unless somebody tells you what the truth of your being is?"

This is the second-and-only question that really matters in life: *Who does Jesus say that I am?*

Shattered Mirrors

Over breakfast with a close friend, he tells me about his struggle to persevere in a job he doesn't like and that will never pay him enough to keep his head above water. He wants to quit, but he has a large family to take care of, and it would be financial suicide for them if he did. He's tried other things that are a better fit for his soul and promise the possibility of better money, but nothing has worked out. He sees himself as a failure—as a man who just doesn't have what it takes. He wonders why God hasn't come through for him, and he suspects the answer to that question is his own inability to trust and believe in God and exercise the courage to step out in faith. His interior conversation is brutally critical because the mirror he's staring at to assess himself is distorted by lies.

I've had this conversation before with my friend, and with many others who have admitted a similar interior conversation. It's hard to talk someone out of a critical assessment of his core identity. We are quick to trust our self-critique because we assume that whatever our assessment might be, it's the most brutally honest mirror. We believe that others, because they default to "polite," will always play spin-doctor with their true experience of us. And so we secretly believe that we're always fooling people into buying a false and better version of ourselves. Therefore, if we're hiding what's true about us from everyone, we assume that all other assessments outside of our own are false. My friend is a deeply honest person, so he's self-aware enough to believe that he's spinning himself all the time. And if you're spinning the reality about who you are all the time, then *only you* really know the bitter truth about yourself. Right?

It's hard to talk someone out of a critical assessment of his core identity.

So I tell my friend that he should never trust his own bad opinion of himself—it's dangerous and wrong. And he asks, "Why did God create us this way?" And I tell him that we've been created fearfully and wonderfully, but sin's fundamental effect has shattered and distorted the mirror we have embedded in our soul. It's a mirror designed to reflect back to us who we really are, but it's not describing the truth about who we are. That voice you have inside, the one that speaks to you with a tone that is dismissive and dripping in cynicism, is your shattered mirror. Every person you know has one.

In Jesus we have a mirror we can trust—he will reflect our true identity back to us directly.

And this is why Jesus is our only trustworthy mirror. We're all wired to discover who we are by looking at mirrors outside ourselves, but the only safe mirror is Jesus. The rest are just as flawed and shattered as our own. In Jesus we have a mirror we can trust—he will reflect our true identity back to us directly. And Jesus will also identify our true self *indirectly* through the Body of Christ, when its corporate reflection dovetails with what he's already revealing about us. I mean, Jesus has chosen to move through his Body, and that means he can artfully piece together the shattered mirrors of his people to give us a reflection of our soul that matches his own direct reflection. What Jesus says about us, and how he sees us, is our only sure foundation—all other reflections will either build on that foundation or tear it down.

Paul says: "Now the Lord is the Spirit, and where the Spirit of the Lord is, there is liberty. But we all, with unveiled face, beholding as in a mirror the glory of the Lord, are being transformed into the same image from glory to glory, just as from the Lord, the Spirit" (2 Corinthians 3:17-18). When we look into the mirror of Jesus, we are transformed by what we see in ourselves. When we move Jesus from the background of our everyday activities into the foreground, we can see ourselves in his mirror more clearly. He releases our true identity from all the false things we, and others, try to pin on us. And he slowly, surely rebuilds the shattered mirror inside us, so that one day our self-assessment will look a lot like his own.

The Truth About You

In his letter to the Ephesians, Paul tells us a bedrock truth: "It's in Christ that we find out who we are and what we are living for" (Ephesians 1:11, The Message). Brennan Manning—author, speaker, former priest, and pied-piper for the "ragamuffin Christian" movement—echoes Paul's declaration in his book *Abba's Child*: "Define yourself radically as one beloved of God. This is the true self. Every other identity is an illusion."[1]

I have a longtime friend who's been mulling the implications of that Brennan Manning quote as he slogs through a long season of struggle and self-doubt. Years ago I'd given him my book *Sifted*, which explores the way Jesus moves through our pain to transform us into people who can bring life-giving strength to the broken and grieving through our deepening attachment to Jesus. The book reflects the truth that the end result of our freedom from captivity is that we can embrace the true identity that Jesus longs to reveal in us. Through our pain, and the healing that follows, we open ourselves to Jesus identifying our core self.

Not long ago my friend wrote me a long email, describing the nooks and crannies of his struggle to understand and embrace the beauty of who he really is. That Brennan Manning quote, he told me, now drills deeper into his soul than it had before. He's been haunted by his inability to define himself radically as one beloved of God, and questions whether he has anything of substance to offer others. This is the kind of internal struggle only people who've traveled through a dark night of the soul have. My friend has not only traveled there, he's camped in its depths.

In *Sifted* I describe a visceral dream that seemed so real to me that after I woke I had to reorient myself to reality. In it, I see myself on a lonely hill with mountains looming in the background. I'm alone in this wilderness, until I see a group of men galloping toward me on horseback. Riding at the front of their column is Jesus, who intends to invite me into the adventure of his mission. In his note to me, my friend injects himself into that scene and imagines what role he would play if he was there with me:

In your dream you see Jesus mounted on a horse, surrounded by other riders, inviting you to join Him on His adventures. Hand outstretched to you, He says: "Mount up, son. I want you to ride with me." And so you pull your awkward self up into the saddle and hang on for dear life. Then, perhaps as you look around at the others Jesus has assembled there on that hill ("they had the look of men who could be counted on"), you see a horse with a near-lifeless body draped, face down, over it. The guy is barely breathing. To keep him from sliding off they have duct-taped him to the animal. They used a whole roll of duct tape. Sadly comical.

Worried, you ask Jesus, "Um, Lord, what is that, that…mess?"

Jesus says, "Oh, he's with me."

"But, he's bleeding all over the saddle. I'm pretty sure he's dead."

"He's not dead," says Jesus.

"He can't even hold a sword. What possible good could he be to us?"

"I told you, he's with me."

You look around at the other trustworthy riders. They just shrug as if to say: "Don't ask us. He made us duct-tape the guy onto the horse." And then you all wheel off and charge down the hill into the great unknown.

I confess there were times I didn't feel I could even be duct-taped to a horse. I felt more like the horse-[manure] on the trail the riders would stomp through on their way to wherever the heck they were going.

In the last chapter of Sifted you quote Luke 19: "(He) came to seek and save what was lost." Thank God for that. If you are going to have Jesus and a bunch of guys roaring in on horses save someone, you gotta have someone to save.

Embedded in my friend's note to me is an overarching truth about all of us, not just those of us who feel like we'd have to be duct-taped to a horse if we have any hope of adventuring with Jesus. At the core of who we really are—the most basic truth about our identity—is this: "He's with me." More than our accomplishments and failures and gifts and irritations, we are defined by what Jesus says about us, and by his determination to reclaim us and include us in his kingdom-of-God life. When he says, "You're with me," that's all we, or anyone else, need to know. We find ourselves in him.

At the core of who we really are—the most basic truth about our identity—is this: "He's with me."

Jesus wants us to know what he sees in us—what he knows is true about us. He is unwilling for us to live under the shadow of a lie about who we really are. And so, as we name the truth about him, he names the truth about us. My friend Ned Erickson once shared with me something he calls "The Progression." It profoundly captures the spirit of this name-him/he-names-us rhythm—it goes like this:

"Get to know Jesus well, because the more you know him, the more you'll love him, and the more you love him, the more you'll want to follow him, and the more you follow him, the more you'll become like him, and the more you become like him, the more you become yourself."[2]

Endnotes

1 Brennan Manning, *Abba's Child: The Cry of the Heart for Intimate Belonging* (Colorado Springs, CO: NavPress, 2002), 60.

2 Ned Erickson learned this progression from his ministry partners in Young Life.

—*Part Two*—
The Beeline Practices

If "understand and apply" and "try harder to get better" have little to do with real transformation, then it does no good to offer a new set of tips and techniques that promise to lead us to a deeper life with Jesus. Unless, of course, we learn to nudge our life in ways that intentionally draw us more deeply into relationship with Jesus—the simple focus of our life habits shifts from working harder to be a better Christian or becoming a good person, to knowing Jesus more intimately. And by knowing him much better, we eventually know ourselves much better—that's what "The Progression" reveals.

Know Him	Love Him	Follow Him	Become Like Him	Become Yourself
J.	J.	J.	J.	J.

Of course, we need strength to experience transformation in our life— but where does that strength come from? If we believe it must come from our own ability to discipline ourselves into maturity, we're headed for shipwreck. But if we embrace the truth that we need strength, and instead look to Jesus to provide it as we attach and re-attach ourselves to the Vine, then the strength we need comes from our dependence, not our independence.

So, what if there's a simple way of living, a way of "practicing" our life, that inexorably draws us closer to Jesus' orbit, enough that we can no longer escape his gravitational pull? What if we replace the 543 "must-do's" of the Christian life with only one thing? *One thing.* Where have we heard that before? Let's revisit this familiar story again...

When Martha of Bethany invites a tired, hungry, and thirsty Jesus into her home, she quickly fixates on the duties of a good host, making sure she serves Jesus well. But her sister Mary is apparently oblivious to Martha's sense of obligation. Instead, she is "seated at the Lord's feet, listening to His word." Martha pleads with Jesus to demand that her sister take her blinders off and help. Instead, Jesus gently rebukes his good friend with this: "Martha, Martha, you are worried and bothered about many things; but only one thing is necessary, for Mary has chosen the good part, which shall not be taken away from her" (Luke 10:38-42).

But if we embrace the truth that we need strength, and instead look to Jesus to provide it as we attach and re-attach ourselves to the "Vine," then the strength we need comes from our dependence, not our independence.

Mary has chosen the one thing, the only thing that's really necessary in life. And what is she choosing against? Well, the important work of a good hostess, at the moment. And why does she make this choice? Certainly *not* because she is shoulded into it—quite the opposite, actually. Mary chooses the only necessary thing in life because she is fascinated by, hungry for, and gravitationally pulled toward Jesus. She has chosen to lay down an activity that will underscore and express her own goodness to, instead, pay close attention to Goodness itself. She has taken a brief Sabbath from trying harder to get better so that she can channel all her attention into knowing Jesus more deeply. She is, as Paul will be later, determined to know nothing but Jesus Christ.

When we prioritize abiding in Jesus because we have been captured by his magnetic beauty, then the practice of our life is continually drawing us closer to him. And when we're always getting a little bit closer to Jesus, we understand why Mary appears so rude and insensitive to her sister—she simply couldn't take her eyes off of Jesus. And that's just another way of saying that her life now orbits around him. She is a pig, not a chicken. And that means Jesus is the constant reference point for everything she does in life, creating in her the blinder effect that so frustrates her sister while simultaneously delighting Jesus.

An object that orbits another is called a satellite. The shape of an orbit is never perfectly circular—it's always elliptical, like an oval.

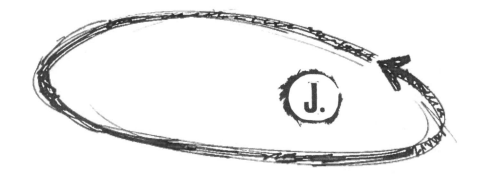

Jesus at the center means that our elliptical orbit in life might feel sometimes near and sometimes far from him, but everything in our lives is nevertheless influenced by his gravitational pull.

Sometimes the orbiting object, the satellite, is closer to its sun, and other times it is farther away. But it never stops orbiting, no matter how far the ellipsis takes it. It reminds me of how Bono, U2's iconic singer/songwriter, responded to a *Rolling Stone* writer's question about his favorite music: "The music that really turns me on is either running toward God or away from God. Both recognize the pivot, that God is at the center of the jaunt."[1] Jesus at the center means that our elliptical orbit in life might feel sometimes near and sometimes far from him, but everything in our lives is nevertheless influenced by his gravitational pull.

Newton's first law of motion says an object in motion stays in motion unless something pushes or pulls on it. So without gravity, an earth-orbiting satellite would career off into space following a straight line. But under the force of the earth's gravitational pull, the satellite is continuously pulled back toward earth. There is a constant tug-of-war between the satellite's tendency to move in a straight line, away from the earth, and the tug of gravity that is pulling the satellite back. In order to achieve orbit, a satellite must have a balanced relationship between the force of gravity that is pulling it down and the force of its forward momentum that keeps it always moving sideways. "Orbital velocity" is the speed a satellite needs to achieve orbit. This means that we need forward momentum in our relationship with Jesus, combined with the magnetic way he draws us to himself, to live a life centered on him.

In Part 2 of *The Jesus-Centered Life*, we'll explore a lifestyle of forward momentum that will make continuous intimacy with him possible—it's a lifestyle of one-thing habits that I call the "Beeline Practices." These are everyday ways of living your life that will help you achieve and maintain an orbit around Jesus, and answer *the only two questions that really matter*: "Who do you say that Jesus is?" and "Who does Jesus say that you (and all those within your sphere of influence) are?"

Almost a decade ago my friend Greg Stier, founder and president of Dare 2 Share Ministries, introduced me to the word "beeline" and the man who first used it to describe the Jesus-centered life. During a break at a day-long gathering of ministry leaders, I was telling Greg about my explorations into what a centered approach to life with Jesus might look like, and he said: "You know, Spurgeon said that no matter what Bible text he was preaching on or what issue he was teaching about, he always made a beeline to the cross, to Jesus."

No matter what he was preaching or teaching or talking about, Spurgeon was always headed toward Jesus.

I'd heard the name Spurgeon before, but had no idea who he was. And *beeline* is an odd word—I needed a little context. So Greg took two minutes to introduce Charles Haddon Spurgeon to me, and that began a long and eye-opening relationship with "the prince of preachers." During the Victorian era, he was one of the most well-known people in the world. Spurgeon pastored the "it" church of his day—New Park Street Chapel in London. At just 22 he was already famous for his remarkable and captivating sermons. Every Sunday he'd preach twice, to congregations of 6,000 people, before the days of microphones and amplification. Today, he still has more books in print than any pastor in history, including more than 2,500 published sermons. Spurgeon lived by a simple burning conviction: to beeline everything in his life and ministry to Jesus. That means that no matter what he was preaching or teaching or talking about, Spurgeon was always headed toward Jesus.

Once, a young pastor asked Spurgeon (now an older man) to critique his preaching, and the great man was blunt: "That was a poor sermon." When the young man asked for an explanation, Spurgeon replied: "Because there was no Christ in it." The young man protested that his chosen Scripture verse had nothing to do with Jesus. And Spurgeon responded: "Don't you know, young man, that from every town, and every village, and every little hamlet in England, wherever it may be, there is a road to London? And so from *every text* in Scripture there is a road to the metropolis of the Scriptures, that is Christ."[2]

Spurgeon's passion for Jesus, and his determination to track everything he said and did back to the metropolis of Christ, describes the forward momentum of a Jesus-centered orbit. Like riding a bike for the first time, these beeline practices will require a little transition time for you to find your balance. But once you learn how your forward velocity on the bike makes it possible to stay perched on it, living in these practices will seem as autonomic as breathing. The satellite doesn't have to work at its orbit once it's achieved. It can't stop orbiting.

The bad news is that the tips-and-techniques that promise to make you a better person aren't going to solve your life. The good news is that the recognition of this truth opens the door to living a beelined life—a life that moves you closer and closer to the intimacy with God that we were created to enjoy.

The fallacy of "try harder to get better" is *not* that we are expending effort in our relationship with Jesus—the problem is that our effort is invested in the self-reclamation project of a dying, disconnected branch, not the fruit-producing effort of a branch that is now abiding in the Vine. Our effort is the passionate outward expression of a life centered on Jesus, not the *source* of our transformation. As we abide in him, Jesus invites us to spend our strength on behalf of our beloved. Put another way, now that we know Oprah a lot better, wouldn't it be fun to cook with her? Let's see what new recipes we can come up with together. But we don't bypass the first-things-first part of the relationship by treating Oprah as if she was merely a recipe-dispenser. For those in intimate relationship, working and playing together is the same as making music together.

Our effort is the passionate outward expression of a life centered on Jesus, not the *source* of our transformation.

The bookend to Paul's first admonition to the believers in Corinth—"I have determined to know nothing among you except Jesus Christ, and Him crucified" (1 Corinthians 2:2)—is this challenge to spend themselves as a result of their abiding: "But just as you abound in everything, in faith and utterance and knowledge and in all earnestness and in the love we inspired in you, see that you abound in this gracious work also" (2 Corinthians 8:7). The "gracious work" that is the fruit of our centered relationship with Jesus has the power to change lives—our own and others. It's best expressed by what Thom and Joani Schultz call "The Four Acts of Love" in their groundbreaking book *Why Nobody Wants to Go to Church Anymore*. These acts of love, pouring forth from a ruined-for-Jesus heart, include:

1. **Radical Hospitality**—Living in an invitational way, serving Jesus and others by relating to them with an acute attention to detail and a childlike spirit of generosity.

2. **Fearless Conversation**—Talking to Jesus, and to others, in the spirit of the Stockdale Paradox (where we face brutal realities while never letting go of our hope). When we live with a commitment to fearless engagement, we pursue to understand, ask more and better questions, and trust that the Spirit of Jesus will guide us.

3. **Genuine Humility**—Opening ourselves to learn in every context, in every way, leads to a lifestyle of pliability. I mean, when we follow Paul's admonition in Romans 12 to never think more highly of ourselves than we ought to think, we're eager to grow and serve.

4. **Divine Anticipation**—Recognizing that Jesus is real, not an idea or a concept or a mythic figure, means that we expect real things to happen in our relationship with him. We anticipate Jesus saying and doing things in our lives today, this moment, trusting his Spirit to guide us in the most mundane aspects of our day.[3]

That's all the Beeline Practices are— playground equipment for the Jesus-centered life.

In one way or another, all of the Beeline Practices you're about to experience fit into one of these four broad categories. *Treat them as a menu of opportunity, not a list of imperatives.* Let's say you were a child again, and you've just arrived at a vast playground with new and exciting slides and monkey bars and castle-like thingies you've never tried before. You'd never treat this sort of nirvana as if it were a to-do list—no, you'd climb on the first available thing and start, well, *playing*. That's all the Beeline Practices are—playground equipment for the Jesus-centered life. Maybe you'll try the tire swing and discover you don't like it as much as the seesaw. There are no *shoulds* here—just opportunities to play. You're right now on the edge of the sandpit, and you'll have a long, long time (an eternity, really) to try out the new playground and find your favorites.

In addition, I've invited some friends—most of them members of a loose collective of Jesus-lovers called the Simply Jesus Gathering—to describe their own playground equipment in little snippets scattered throughout the remainder of this book. I asked them to simply offer what they do to keep Jesus at the center of their orbit. I'm grateful they've offered to give us all a peek into their own daily beeline practices.

Endnotes

1 From a *Rolling Stone* interview of Bono, November 3, 2005 (No. 986).

2 Taken from Sermon 242, *Christ Precious to Believers*, preached by Charles Spurgeon on March 13, 1859.

3 Thom Schultz and Joani Schultz, *Why Nobody Wants to Go to Church Anymore: And How 4 Acts of Love Will Make Your Church Irresistible* (Loveland, CO: Group Publishing, 2013).

8

Entering the Thicker Life

"God did not create us to live in reaction, but to be co-creators of a meaningful life."

—Viktor Frankl

In your home, where would you go if you wanted to brainstorm something or discover a deep insight? Well, there's only one real choice, according to researchers—your shower or bathtub is, by far, the prime hunting ground for creative thinking. And why is this true? Because, so far, your shower and bathtub remain toxic environments for digital devices. And our digital devices have accelerated our exposure to a virus that has spread faster and impacted more lives than any other in world history—it's called distraction. We live in the age of distraction, and it's creating a *thinness of soul* in us. Distraction causes a different kind of heart disease—our souls' arteries get clogged with a kind of plaque buildup that an overwhelming engagement with our cultural inputs produces.

Joe Kraus is a highly successful tech entrepreneur, a partner in the venture capital firm Google Ventures, and a board member for the Electronic Frontier Foundation—he has the DNA of a digital apologist. And yet, in a public presentation that created a stir in his industry, Kraus outed himself as a distraction junkie:

Are you happy with your relationship with your phone? Do you think it's a healthy one? I don't think I have a healthy relationship with mine. I feel a constant need to pull it out—to check email, to text, to see if there is something interesting happening RIGHT NOW. It's constantly pulling on my attention… We are creating and encouraging a culture of distraction where we are increasingly disconnected from the people and events around us and increasingly unable to engage in long-form thinking. People now feel anxious when their brains are unstimulated. We are losing some very important things by doing this. We threaten the key ingredients behind creativity and insight by filling up all our "gap" time with stimulation. And we inhibit real human connection when we prioritize our phones over the people right in front of us.[1]

The over-stimulated life, where we never meet a gap in time that can't be filled with a ready distraction, is also impacting a critical relationship that *must* have gap time to survive: our relationship with God. In *Death by Suburb,* author Dave Goetz advocates a countercultural way of living that he calls "the thicker life."[2] This kind of lifestyle is marked by a slowed-down and singular pursuit of Jesus, an everyday dependence on his guidance, and a pattern of noticing and serving the needs of others. To live this way, we would need to adopt a more focused, less scattered mindset. "Thick" is a slow-down-and-pay-attention way of life, and it's in stark contrast to the speed-up-and-distract-myself way of life that's the norm in our culture.

We know that thick is better for our souls than thin, but we often feel helpless to do anything about it.

Filling Up the Cracks

Viktor Frankl, an Austrian psychologist and Holocaust survivor, emerged from his horrific experiences as a slave laborer in a concentration camp with a determined conviction that human beings, at their core, hunger for meaning in life. His book, *Man's Search for Meaning,* written in 1946, just a year after his liberation, was named by the Library of Congress as one of the 10 most influential books in U.S. history. In it, Frankl contends that a meaningless life is intolerable, and those who fail to find their deeper purpose compensate by numbing themselves with pleasure. Meaning, he said, is tied to our commitment to serve others, our ability to nurture intimate relationships, and our redemptive attitude toward suffering.[3] These building blocks of meaning are directly tied to the thicker life—those who live in the frenetic chaos of distraction can't offer the right soil for meaning to grow in their souls. A reactive life, like the surface of the moon, can't provide the right conditions for abundant life to take hold and thrive. And Jesus came to plant *life* in us: "The thief comes only to steal and kill and destroy; I came that they may have life, and have it abundantly" (John 10:10).

Most people fear boredom more than any other everyday threat.

Analyzing our behavior in Western culture, we must conclude that most people fear boredom more than any other everyday threat. Like mortar between bricks, we fill up our empty spaces with boredom-beating distractions. We pour information and interaction into our crevices. Digital connections fuel our hyper-stimulating lives, changing how our brains are wired. New research on the impact of our technology connections reveals startling differences in brain functioning. According to researchers Nathaniel Barr and Gordon Pennycook of the University of Waterloo's psychology department: "Although the tendency to seek knowledge and information is often equated with intelligence, cognitive ability [is] associated with less smartphone use and less time spent using online search engines."[4] In other words, the less connected we are, the more brainpower and insight we gain, because we have the empty space to chew and consider and live more...thickly.

Could it be that the bricks that make up the structure of our lives need less, not more, mortar between them? That doesn't seem intuitive or even plausible, and yet something in us knows that we're living as if we're rocks skipping across the surface of a lake. We know we're not sinking very deeply into the depths of life, so we're vulnerable to the shifting social and emotional forces that surround us. Our mounting lack of depth makes us reactive by default and eats away at our foundation, making it easier to topple.

The thicker life is only possible if we slow down to drill more deeply into our most important truths. I mean, it's not possible to speed-date our way to a more intimate relationship with Jesus and others.

I mean, it's not possible to speed-date our way to a more intimate relationship with Jesus and others.

So to live a thicker life, we walk the (digital) road less traveled, not because there is anything inherently wrong with the tools we are using, but because the way we use these tools is profoundly undermining our most important pursuits in life. A chainsaw is just a tool—without it, we'd have no wood to construct our homes. But we'd also have no *Texas Chainsaw Massacre*. Powerful tools require greater attention in how we use them, because they can build or destroy. Our digital distractions, of course, are just the current iteration of a permanent challenge—we have always been people who abhor a vacuum, and we have always been people who try to fill our vacuums with something that can distract us. "Digital" is just a contemporary placeholder for our latest source of distraction. All of life is a continuously accelerating engine of distraction.

"I go for a long run, put on the headphones, and listen to a podcast or worship music, then think and talk it out with Jesus." —Jo Saxton

And the thicker life, the life that gives us access to the relational treasures we *really* want, is possible only when we keep some of our gaps, not fill all of them. To live a slowed-down life, we'll need to find slow in the midst of fast. We'll need to find simple in the midst of complex. But we all know that if we slow down in the fast lane, we're likely to get run off the road. So, what would it look like to inject *slow* into our *fast*, in a seamless way? For starters, how about some countercultural habits that replace thin with thick in our lives...

1. **Live with a Sabbath mentality.** In the Western world, we have
   made Sabbath a day instead of a lifestyle. When God rested on the
   seventh day of Creation, he was modeling a lifestyle, not a rigid
   formula. But when you're always moving fast, slow is always an
   irritation. So whenever I have to wait for anything, instead of turning
   to a distraction to fill the gap, I tell myself (usually out loud, laughing
   at myself) that I've been given the gift of a contemplative moment. It's
   a wry joke, and a reminder and an invitation to enter into Sabbath.
   So I resist the urge to distract myself in that waiting room moment
   and, instead, pause to ask a silent question and then listen:

   What is troubling me right now, Jesus?

   Where do I feel fear in my life right now, Jesus?

   What have I forgotten to thank you for, Jesus?

   What do you want me to know about you, Jesus?

   What do you want me to know about myself, Jesus?

   What's going on in my heart right now, Jesus?

   Who or what do I need to pay attention to right now, Jesus?

   Really, any question about who Jesus is, or who I am, is a perfect
   Sabbath-moment question. These are rooted in the two broad questions
   that Jesus has set out for us: "Who do I say Jesus is?" and "Who does
   Jesus say I am?" We ask, and we rest for a moment as we listen.

   Alternately, I leave the contemplative moments blank—I give
   my racing mind a rest. You know how a blank stare has negative
   connotations? Well, maybe our Sabbath moments invite blank
   stares. Find something to stare at through a window, or study one
   detail of the room you're in. Or simply stare into space for a few
   moments. Rest. These moments are mini-Sabbaths that can plunge
   us into the rhythms of God. If a gap moment is an invitation to a
   45-second Sabbath—a place of rest or gentle inquiry for our mind,
   will, and emotions—then our response to that invitation can be
   subtly courageous: "No, I will leave this gap unfilled." Enter into
   the gap with *nothing*, and let *nothing* give your soul rest. Enjoy what
   bubbles to the surface when you still the waters of your mind, even
   for a moment.

"The busier I am, the more I need to take time to be quiet, to pray, and to read the Bible. Sometimes I do this when things aren't so quiet—while driving, while cutting grass, or while trimming my nails. But I believe it gives him the opportunity to speak to me, to direct me, to encourage me, and to let me know he cares about my stuff. He delights in even me." —Phil Callaway

2. **Notice, notice, notice.** Socrates reminds us that "the life that is unexamined is not worth living."[5] One key to the thicker life is to do what my friend Tom Melton calls "noticing what we notice." What is capturing your thoughts, your eyes, your nose, or your ears in your gap moments? You'll have to slow down, just a little, to notice what you notice. Just becoming aware of your inner life, or your senses, is enough to open the door to a slow-in-the-midst-of-fast contemplation. But the thicker life means that we invite Jesus into these spaces. Tell Jesus what you're thinking or feeling or hearing or seeing or smelling, and then ask him a simple question: *What do you think about that?* or *Why am I noticing that right now?* or *What's true and not true about that?* or *Where are you in that?* or *Why am I reacting this way?* Expect him to respond, and he will.

If we're not paying close attention to what motivates us, and what motivates others, we'll never dip below the surface in any relationship. Because beauty is always in the details, we'll have to notice the details of others to draw out their beauty.

What emotions do I pick up in this person, and why?

How is this person impacting me right now?

What is unique about the way I'm experiencing this person right now?

What's something about this person that reminds me of Jesus right now?

Perhaps our deepest longing as human beings is to be enjoyed for our beauty, and few have ever had anyone see through the wall of distractions to mark the details of their beauty. Few of us ever feel noticed. Even fewer feel *ridiculously* noticed. If you will do this as an act of worship, you will participate with Jesus in setting captives free.

If we're not paying close attention to what motivates us, and what motivates others, we'll never dip below the surface in any relationship.

---

3. **Follow the beeline.** If our mindset is always to read the Bible as if we are on a Jesus-safari, looking for him behind every tree and bush, then we'll find ourselves slowing down to taste and see him no matter what part of the Bible we're reading. This was my team's driving mission when we created the *Jesus-Centered Bible*—how can we highlight and reveal Jesus throughout the Bible, not just where we expect to find him? For example, we found and highlighted close to 700 places in the Old Testament that point to Jesus or connect to Jesus in some way—we made those passages blue, to complement the red letters in the New Testament that mark Jesus' words. And we added little caption-boxes next to the highlighted passages to explain the connection. The impact of this is a closer orbit around Jesus as we read, no matter where we read.

If we keep our Jesus-curious switch always on, we're constantly wondering how any random passage points to Jesus or prepares us for Jesus or helps us understand Jesus better. The effect of finding the beeline to Jesus every time we crack open the Bible (or tap on our Bible app) is that we learn to follow every road until we end up in the metropolis of Christ. We clear our distractions by paying attention to Jesus, no matter where we're reading in the Bible. And when we find him, we chew on him. The simple questions that lead us there:

How does this story or truth connect to the heart of Jesus or the truths he has revealed?

What about this story or truth reminds me of Jesus?

How does this story or truth match, or not match, my experience of Jesus?

If I was going to teach someone the meaning of this story or truth, how would I connect it to Jesus?

After the first few times you use this filter as you read, you'll find your switch is turned on, permanently.

4. **Switch off/switch on.** Slow down your inner flywheel in the middle of a rushed life with subtle and simple substitutions. For example:

• Switch off your lights at home and light candles instead. Lit candles are soothing, and the light they provide has an invitational impact on the soul. The amber warmth of candlelight simplifies your environment by highlighting only a few things in the foreground while masking the rest of your environment in the background. The subdued light creates relaxed space for your brain; it has less stimulation to process. And flame is fundamental to human beings— it's organic light, not artificial, so it's like giving your soul fresh fruit to eat instead of canned fruit.

In the '50s people laughed, on average, 18 minutes a day—but today that's dwindled to six minutes a day.

• Switch off the news or DJ-driven show on your radio when you're driving for two or three minutes and pray out loud instead. Treat your prayer like an audio diary, and spill out to Jesus what you're thinking and feeling. Or simply be quiet for those minutes. Notice the clock on your dashboard, and shut down your audio stimulation for a predetermined length (at least two minutes, but less than five) by simply marking the time. Or switch the radio to a quieter music station that's free of screaming DJs and leave it there for the rest of your trip. Alternatively, switch it to a comedy station on Sirius or one of the NPR humor/storytelling shows (*Car Talk* or *Wait, Wait, Don't Tell Me* or *This American Life*). In the '50s people laughed, on average, 18 minutes a day—but today that's dwindled to six minutes a day.[6] We're suffering from a laughter drought, and that means we're missing God's natural antidepressant. He's wired us to enjoy laughter as a natural release of the tension that builds from our breakneck lives. Give your soul less work to do, and find ways for it to play instead.

• Switch off the TV as background noise to some portion of your day (especially the evening), and switch on music for the soul instead. In our home (that includes two teenagers) we prefer old-school jazz/R&B/blues. But worship music, or almost any genre of instrumental music, is also a great alternative. If these options make you wince, find a style of music that brings *rest*, not acceleration, to your soul. Or simply opt for a brief vacation from sensory stimulation and keep your audio background quiet for a predetermined time.

• Switch off all technology in your home during stretches of no-noise time, leaving empty space for focused conversation. I have a close friend who is super-connected to her technologies, but whenever she's with friends or family and the point is to have a conversation, you won't see her digital devices anywhere near her. She clears her distractions so she can focus on the person. And even though everyone in her family also uses digital devices, they all put them aside during family time.

• Switch off the car ignition and walk, whenever possible, instead. Walking is not only physically healthy for us, it has an even bigger impact on slowing down our flywheel. It's hard not to be dragged into a rush mentality when we're driving, and it's likewise hard to feel rushed when we're walking, even if we're walking to an appointment or to work or to get on the subway. We were born with legs—every other mode of transportation is a device. Use fewer devices and you'll slow down, just a little. This is not Amish-extreme living, but ask someone living in Amish community about the benefits of device-less living, and they'll offer a treatise.

The thicker life, or a life seasoned by restful moments, reorients us away from a "doing" identity to a "being" identity. Old Testament scholar Walter Brueggemann says: "Sabbath, in the first instance, is not about worship. It is about work stoppage. It is about...the refusal to let one's life be defined by production and consumption and the endless pursuit of private well-being."[7] Entering into our micro-Sabbath moments in the middle of the fast lane honors our hearts, because the heart is not defined by what it produces—it is defined by what it loves. Do this, and you'll create space to connect with Jesus and maybe even hear his voice on a regular basis.

The thicker life, or a life seasoned by restful moments, reorients us away from a "doing" identity to a "being" identity.

What would happen if your strategies to bring slow into your fast gave you just enough margin to feel just a little closer to Jesus in your everyday life? Well, fruit would happen, because Jesus generates fruit the closer we get to him—"love, joy, peace, patience, kindness, goodness, faithfulness, gentleness, and self-control" (Galatians 5:22-23, NLT).

Endnotes

1 From the blog post "We're Creating a Culture of Distraction," by Joe Kraus (JoeKraus.com, May 25, 2012).

2 Dave Goetz, *Death by Suburb: How to Keep the Suburbs From Killing Your Soul* (New York, NY: HarperCollins, 2007).

3 Victor Frankl, *Man's Search for Meaning* (Boston, MA: Beacon Press, 2006).

4 Quoted in the Washington Post article "Study: Smartphones Replace Thinking," by Justin Wm. Moyer, March 12, 2015.

5 Socrates, quoted in *Apology*, Plato's account of the trial of Socrates, translated by Benjamin Jowett, 37e-38a.

6 From a study led by German psychologist Dr. Michael Titze, referenced in the article "Laugh and Be Well," published on the Environmental News Network website on November 30, 2001.

7 Walter Brueggemann, *Journey to the Common Good* (Louisville, KY: Westminster John Knox Press, 2010), 26.

—9—

Paying Ridiculous Attention to Jesus

"For some of his utterances men might fairly call him a maniac; for others, men long centuries afterwards might justly call him a prophet. But what nobody can possibly call him is Galilean of the time of Tiberius. That was not how he appeared to his own family, who tried to lock him up as a lunatic. That is not how he appeared to his nation, who lynched him, still shuddering at his earth-shaking blasphemies. The impression produced on skeptics, ancient and modern, is not that of limits, but rather of a dangerous absence of limits; a certain shapelessness and mystery of which one cannot say how far it will go."

—G.K. Chesterton

In *Ruthless Trust*, author Brennan Manning writes: "It must be noted that Jesus alone reveals who God is... We cannot deduce anything about Jesus from what we think we know about God; however, we must deduce everything about God from what we know about Jesus."[1] This is just. So. True.

Our inherent misconceptions about God won't help us understand Jesus. But a fascination with the things Jesus says and does will very much help us understand God. The great and enduring question of all of humanity is, simply: "Is there a God, and if there is, what is that God like?" We make our quest to answer this question much more difficult than it needs to be. We assume the deepest questions require the most complex answers. But the answer is actually simple, as long as we follow the path both Brennan Manning and the Apostle Paul have laid out (remember, again, Paul's declaration in 1 Corinthians 2: "For I determined to know nothing among you except Jesus Christ, and Him crucified").

In the Oscar-nominated film *Philomena*, a skeptical investigative journalist agrees to help an aging woman find her lost son—the nuns at a Catholic convent took the boy from her when he was a toddler and gave him to adoptive parents from America. Fifty years later she hasn't stopped looking for him. As a teenager, Philomena was essentially imprisoned in the convent, sent there by her parents after a one-night stand with another teenager left her pregnant. The film is based on a true story, and the British journalist in the story is Martin Sixsmith, who has long-since given up on a God he does not understand or respect or believe in. Philomena, of course, has every reason to raise her fist to a God who allowed her son to be taken from her by the duplicitous representatives of the church. But she nevertheless persists in her love for Jesus. On a long car ride through the English countryside, she bluntly asks Sixsmith, "Do you believe in God, Martin?" And the journalist, caught off-guard, awkwardly responds: "Well, where do you start? That's a very difficult question to answer, isn't it... Umm... do you?" Quickly, Philomena barks back: "Yes!"[2] It's a quietly epic moment, with the bright light of Philomena's childlike certainty cutting through Sixsmith's tired and over-wrought mental fog.

The certain path to "yes" when the question is whether or not God is real, and whether or not he is good, is through the man who declared, "I am the way, the truth, and the life."

The certain path to "Yes!" when the question is whether or not God is real, and whether or not he is good, is through the man who declared, "I am the way, the truth, and the life." And we are living out a beeline practice when we *pay ridiculous attention to Jesus.*

It is through our ridiculous attention to everything Jesus said and did that we discover the truth about God, and the truth about ourselves. We learn everything about God by slowing way down to consider what Jesus actually said and did, who he actually said and did it to, and the actual impact his words and actions had on people. When we let our pursuit of Jesus guide our understanding of God, our lives will be transformed by what we discover.

Jesus tried to make this dynamic clear to his closest friends, urging them to pay ridiculous attention to his words and actions: "Pay close attention to what you hear. The closer you listen, the more understanding you will be given—and you will receive even more. To those who listen to my teaching, more understanding will be given. But for those who are not listening, even what little understanding they have will be taken away from them" (Mark 4:24-25).

"I regularly return to and immerse myself in Jesus' teachings—spoken and lived. When I read the Bible, alone or in a group, I have a sense that the Bible I'm reading is a gift from the body of Christ to me. Believers have preserved, copied, translated, printed, and distributed this Bible in front of me. The words on the page are a translation—the words of the church approximating and mediating the words of Jesus to me—which is as much a point of connection with believers today and long dead as it is a point of connection with Jesus himself. I read, study, pray through, and then meditate on each passage I immerse myself in, in that order." —Bruxy Cavey

So, if Jesus is an exact mirror for God's character and personality, a journey of paying ridiculous attention to Jesus through the whole length of Matthew's Gospel reveals what must also be true about God. In Matthew's account of what Jesus said and did, we discover...

• Jesus spent more time praying than speaking. His dependent relationship with his Father fueled everything he said and did. He honored the intimacy of his one-on-one relationship with his Father above his teaching, his ministry of healing, and his miracle-working.

• Jesus enjoyed spending time with self-confessed sinners—they were some of his best friends on earth. He liked hanging out with people who were not trying to "spin" him. They were simply honest about who they really were, with all their flaws.

• Jesus said we'd know we were starting to make an impact when people started insulting, persecuting, and defaming us because of him. He is not moved or motivated by unfair critique or misplaced abuse. It's impossible to force Jesus to capitulate on the truth—he cannot be pressured into compromising his integrity.

• Jesus hated it when people hid behind religious rule-keeping. His goal is to lead us back into a Garden-of-Eden intimacy in our relationship with him, and formulaic approaches to relationship are disgusting to him.

• Jesus told his followers to plunge themselves into the mainstream culture like a lamp in a dark room or salt added to a recipe. He is not afraid of a culture dominated by sin—in fact, the darkness of the culture only serves to accentuate the impact of his light.

• Jesus spoke openly about hell and warned there are real consequences for those who cling to self-sufficiency and unbelief. God is no pushover, and he's no helicopter parent. God will not rescue us from ourselves when we are determined to go our own way.

• Jesus hated it when people prayed or served or sacrificed to boost their profiles or feed their egos. He honored secret acts because they revealed a desire for an honest relationship with God.

Jesus was quick to forgive those who were repentant and quick to condemn those who weren't.

• Jesus was quick to forgive those who were repentant and quick to condemn those who weren't. He directly ties the magnitude of his forgiveness to the magnitude of our love for him.

• Jesus said the richest people were those who'd banked a lifetime of actions that honored God. He bluntly told his followers they could *not* be motivated by love of money and love of God at the same time.

• Jesus told us to ignore people who talk big but don't act big and to honor those who talk small but act big.

• Jesus spent a great deal of time healing people of incurable diseases and permanent disabilities. His compassion for the broken and broken-hearted is perpetual and deep.

• Jesus spent a great deal of time asserting his authority over demonic spirits and destroying the works of the devil—he was continuously releasing people from the captivity of demonic oppression and possession.

• Jesus loved celebrations and enjoyed himself so much that the religious rule-keepers accused him of public drunkenness.

• Jesus told his disciples that joining him in his redemptive mission would require us to put our "skin in the game"—our personal investment of risk and hard work is conjoined with his own to advance his kingdom. He will not do *for* us what he can do *with* us.

• Jesus said our loyalty to him and his ways should outweigh our loyalty to our biological family and its traditions and practices. We have only one true parent, and God has claimed that title.

• Jesus told us not to focus our energies on fighting sin but instead to do everything we can to encourage good growth. He is less interested in what we're against, and more interested in what we are for.

• Jesus recognized what fantastic forgetters we are and repeatedly urged his followers to listen to him and remember the things he said and did.

These attributes, condensed from what Jesus said and did in Matthew's Gospel, are just scratching the surface of his magnetic personality. The stories about Jesus and his teachings are a well of understanding in our quest to know and understand God—we can lower our bucket into that well over and over and never run out of living water. And when we do lower our bucket, we're not studying to learn his principles; we're studying to *comprehend his heart*.

The great English poet Elizabeth Barrett Browning wrote:

Earth's crammed with heaven.
And every common bush afire with God;
But only he who sees takes off his shoes;
The rest sit round it and pluck blackberries.[3]

The difference between paying attention to the stories and teachings of Jesus as if "every common bush" was "afire with God" and spending our days "sitting round" them and "plucking blackberries" hinges on our curiosity. Curiosity is the natural passion of children, and Jesus framed childlikeness as essential to our life with God: "And He called a child to Himself and set him before them, and said, 'Truly I say to you, unless you are converted and become like children, you will not enter the kingdom of heaven. Whoever then humbles himself as this child, he is the greatest in the kingdom of heaven' " (Matthew 18:2-4). It is genuinely humble to fuel our childlike curiosity—to treat every detail of the things Jesus said and did as a wonder and a revelation and a portal into his heart.

"I approach Scripture as a narrative, not a collection of systems. God is the author, Jesus is the main character, and the Holy Spirit is a daily guide and fellow sojourner." —Steve Merritt

The truly curious slow down and pay eccentric attention to the nuances of these stories, and to the nudges of his Spirit, and then embrace their implications. That's what paying ridiculous attention looks like. Another way of describing what I mean is "mindfulness"—it's a New Age-y word I despised before I fully understood what it meant. But then I heard Ellen Langer, a Harvard psychologist and author of *Mindfulness,* interviewed on NPR's *Talk of the Nation.* She advocates a way of living that has a direct connection to the ridiculous-attention pursuit of Jesus: "When you're being mindful, you're simply noticing new things," says Langer. "Mindfulness is what you're doing when you're at leisure. [For example] if you are on a vacation, you're looking for new things. It's enjoyable rather than taxing. It's mostly energy-begetting, not energy-consuming."[4]

Mindfulness in our approach to Jesus translates to a passion for paying attention to the things he says and does when a kind of numbed disengagement is the more common habit. To use Langer's definition, we simply "notice new things" about him, even (and especially) in stories we've heard since we were children. And we gain energy when we do this, rather than lose it. The rhythm looks like this…

• We take a "vacation" perspective and treat everything we read about Jesus as if it's the first time we've ever experienced it.

• We read or listen to understand his heart, rather than copying down his recipes.

• We ask far more "why" questions about him than we typically ask.

• We never assume we already know what's going on when Jesus is engaging the crowds or his disciples or an individual. Instead, we come to everything with a child's curiosity.

• We recognize, again, that beauty is in the details, so we are always looking for, and chewing on, the details that surround Jesus' behavior—and we let them lead us to a deeper understanding of him.

When we pay ridiculous attention to Jesus, our ridiculous descriptions of him are obliterated, making way for the real Jesus, whose massive gravitational pull will capture us in his orbit.

Endnotes

1 Brennan Manning, *Ruthless Trust* (New York, NY: Harper Collins, 2002), 88.

2 From the shooting script for *Philomena*, written by Steve Coogan and Jeff Pope. Based on the book *The Lost Child of Philomena Lee*, by Martin Sixsmith (London, UK: Pan Books, May 21, 2010).

3 Elizabeth Barrett Browning, "From 'Aurora Leigh' " from *The Oxford Book of English Mystical Verse*, D.H.S. Nicholson & A.H.E. Lee, eds. (New York, NY: Bartleby.Com, 2000), no. 86.

4 Ellen Langer quoted on the National Public Radio show "Talk of the Nation," hosted by Neil Conan, in the segment titled "Mindfulness—Thinking Counter-Clockwise to Relieve Stress" (August 2, 2012).

Wallowing in Mud Puddles

"I thought Christ was like this weird Santa Claus figure. [But my friend told me], 'If you're going to talk about Christ, you should probably read the Gospels, so at least that way, you'll know what you're talking about.' So I did, and I was converted."

—Moby

How do we get to the bottom of Jesus (so to speak)? If our goal is to move away from our lazy-thinking habits—"We kinda sorta already know who Jesus is"—to the beeline habits that encourage us to pay attention more honestly to him, we will stop jumping over "mud puddles" when we read about him in the Bible. So often we treat the hard or confusing or mysterious things Jesus said and did just like mud puddles—when we come to them in Scripture, we just jump over them. Maybe it doesn't *feel* like we jump over them, but we do. We tell ourselves something like: "Well, that's Jesus for you...he's just a mystery." So we don't step into the mud puddles and wallow around until we know him better; we hop over them.

Once, I was leading a group of Bible college students through a deeper exploration of Jesus and his unpredictable behavior. We stopped at one of my favorite mud puddles in the New Testament—it's the story of the Canaanite woman who pleads with Jesus to cast a demonic presence out of her suffering daughter, but she is rejected by him and called a "dog" in the process (Matthew 15:21-28). I asked the students to explore with a partner all the possible reasons why Jesus responded this way. Then I checked in with the pairs to dialogue about their answers. Two young women were clearly upset by the whole assignment. In their back-and-forth with me, they insisted that the Jesus they were encountering in this Bible passage couldn't be the real Jesus. The dialogue, which had grown more and more frustrating for these women, finally ended with one of them saying, "Maybe 'dog' was actually a compliment in that culture.' "

That's jumping over a mud puddle, not wallowing in it.

"I spend a ton of time in the Gospels (Matthew, Mark, Luke, and John). You can't be intimate with someone you don't know, and the Gospels have the most information about Jesus that we have. I read and reread them for every possible angle. I don't only want information, of course, but simple understanding isn't a bad place to begin." —Carl Medearis

If we accept and affirm that Jesus is fundamentally good, and that he is always offering the people around him transformational love, then we lean into these difficult stories until we understand something of their depth. We don't bail out of them with answers that only serve our plausibility structures. What if the ridiculous truth about Jesus' encounter with the Canaanite woman is that he sometimes loves people by provoking their courage—inviting them to emerge from the shadow of their shame and risk trusting in him? We cannot solve the dissonance we feel when we ram into Jesus as he really is by defaulting to our plausible Jesus assumptions. Instead, we wallow in that mud puddle until we've responded to *Who do you say that I am?* with a more considered answer.

The key to understanding Jesus is finding and wallowing in the mud-puddle stories that most confound us.

In fact, the key to understanding Jesus is finding and wallowing in the mud-puddle stories that most confound us. It's in the hard stories that we discover his heart most clearly. So we stay in those stories long enough to consider Jesus more deeply. We follow G.K. Chesterton's piercing advice: "If you meet the Jesus of the Gospels, you must redefine what love is, or you won't be able to stand him."[1] Because Jesus never did anything outside of love, we say to ourselves, "What Jesus said and did here is a perfect expression of love," then work backward from that assumption to understand how love was at work in him. We're determined to look Jesus full in the face—to not shy away from the things he did that make us uncomfortable, confused, or even angry. As we question, we're digging for the truth about Jesus. We don't accept shallow explanations, and we don't move past the confusing or difficult things about Jesus too quickly. We wallow in mud puddles until we know him better.

We're determined to look Jesus full in the face—to not shy away from the things he did that make us uncomfortable, confused, or even angry.

And, if we are living like pigs and not chickens, as people who are giving all and not some of ourselves to Jesus, we'll actually come to love wallowing in him as an everyday habit. For our own good, we get a little dirty in the messes we've subtly avoided before, including this tiny sampler of mudholes:

• **Jesus cursing the fig tree**—Creation is under obedience to its King. We see this when Jesus walks on water, raises Lazarus from the dead, multiplies a small helping of bread and fish, turns water into wine, and on and on. In the presence of Jesus, all of creation must obey its King—to do what he says. But in this case, the fig tree does not, and it is rebuked. It shrivels under the force of this rebuke.

• **Jesus driving the money changers out of the Temple**—At the time of Passover, when 300,000 to 400,000 pilgrims thronged to Jerusalem, visitors to the Temple brought coins from their hometowns, most bearing the images of Roman emperors or Greek gods. The religious leaders condemned these currencies as idolatrous and decreed that only Tyrian shekels would be accepted for the annual Temple tax, because they contained a higher percentage of silver. The money changers exchanged the unacceptable coins for shekels, most often charging a profit that was much more than the law allowed. Jesus' enraged response to this injustice was so intense that he managed to clear the outer courts of all these shysters.

"My daily practice of moments of silence and meditation, when my mind rests and centers in the person of Jesus, helps me listen to his voice. True spirituality comes from within, beneath the skin of religious language and tradition." —Jonathan Salgado

• **Jesus calling Peter "Satan"**—Just after Simon Peter names Jesus the Messiah and Son of the living God, marking his true identity for the first time, he reprimands Jesus for insisting that he's about to be killed. Jesus, in turn, blasts Peter with this: "Get away from me, Satan! You are a dangerous trap to me" (Matthew 16:23, NLT).

• **Jesus telling the rich young ruler all his efforts are not enough to inherit eternal life**—To a young man who has doggedly followed the precise dictates of Jewish religious law his whole life, Jesus raises the bar even higher: "There is still one thing you haven't done. Sell all your possessions and give the money to the poor, and you will have treasure in heaven. Then come, follow me" (Luke 18:22, NLT).

Wallowing means we stop and roll around in these stories, asking ourselves these questions until we emerge from the puddle with a better understanding of Jesus' heart:

• **What did Jesus really say/do here?** Don't ask, "What *would* Jesus do?" Instead, ask: "What *did* Jesus do?" The first tries to predict something that's unpredictable. The second is simply getting to know Jesus better.

• **When did he say/do it?** Think about the timing of what's happening—put yourself in the shoes of someone who heard or saw him, and consider the context.

• **Where did this all happen?** Consider the physical and geographical setting where Jesus said and did these things. How would that change your surface understanding of him in this situation? Of course, Bible commentaries offer this kind of detail, but an Internet search engine is a quick alternative. What did the surroundings look like when Jesus stepped from a boat onto the beach and was confronted by the Gerasene demoniac? Wikipedia can give you a 30-second overview.

• **What are all the possible reasons he said/did this?** Think through some likely explanations for Jesus' behavior, without defaulting to your preconceptions. Then ask yourself which explanation is consistent with transformative, not transactional, love. Assume whatever he did or said was the most loving thing he could do in that moment, and consider him in that light.

Assume whatever he did or said was the most loving thing he could do in that moment, and consider him in that light.

• **How did he say/do this?** Consider the tone and emotional context of Jesus' behavior—we often don't get that context from the Scripture itself, so we have to pay attention to nuances we normally wouldn't consider. What if Jesus said it with a big smile on his face instead of the scowl we assume he has? What if he said it while laughing or crying? Or what if he said it with a tone of irony?

When we wallow in mud puddles, we remind ourselves that everything Jesus does is subject to love—to the brokenhearted he's a balm, to the hypocritical he's their worst nightmare. But the purpose, either way, is to set captives free. There is no story about Jesus that won't lead us to his heart, if we will wallow long enough.

Endnotes

1 G.K. Chesterton, quoted in *The Everyman Chesterton* (Everyman's Library, 2001), in the "front matter," page xviii.

Asking the Oprah Question

"[St. Paul] knew nothing of the so-called Christian systems that change the glory of the perfect God into the likeness of the low intellects and dull consciences of men—a worse corruption than the representing of him in human shape... Jesus Christ is the only likeness of the living Father."

—George MacDonald

On a Monday morning in the summer of 1899, longtime newspaper editor Louis Klopsch was laboring over his editorial for the next issue of *The Christian Herald*, a monthly with a quarter-of-a-million subscribers. He stopped to wrestle with something Jesus said to his disciples in the middle of The Last Supper (Luke 22:20): "This cup which is poured out for you is the new covenant in My blood." A possibility surfaced in his imagination: *What if the words of Jesus took on the color of his blood, symbolizing his great sacrifice on our behalf?* Klopsch turned to his spiritual mentor Thomas De Witt Talmage, one of the most respected pastors of the late 19th century, and asked him what he thought about publishing a Bible with the words of Jesus highlighted in red. Talmage replied, "It could do no harm and it most certainly could do much good."[1]

This is the moment of conception for the "Red-Letter Bible"—a version of the Bible that debuted to instant popularity and remains popular even today. Later, Klopsch explained his passion for this simple but profound addition to Scripture-reading: "In the Red Letter Bible, more clearly than in any other edition of the Holy Scriptures, it becomes plain that from beginning to end, the central figure upon which all lines of law, history, poetry and prophecy converge is Jesus Christ, the Saviour of the world."

Red is not only symbolic of the shed blood of Jesus, it's also the most arresting color in the palette. The brain translates red into "pay attention." This is why stop signs all over the world are always painted red—even if their shapes vary, their color does not. Of course, the whole of the Bible is important to study, but the words of Jesus invite special attention because, as Klopsch recognized, the whole of the Bible's narrative points to him. In a Jesus-centered life, the "red stuff" of the Bible is a call to action—it invites us to give greater focus to the things Jesus actually said.

"I look for unhurried spaces to listen to Jesus—most often it involves some slow-chewing of God's Word." —Dave Rahn

My favorite way to focus on the red stuff in the Bible is to ask "the Oprah Question." Near the back of every *O, The Oprah Magazine* is a celebrity interview including this brilliant question: "What's one thing you know for sure?" Oprah believed so deeply in this question that she published *What I Know For Sure*, a collection of columns extracted and edited from her magazine. As a lifelong journalist myself, I've interviewed hundreds of people over the years, and I think the Oprah Question is the best single interview question I've ever heard. So I co-opted her question, morphing it into this:

"Based on this Scripture passage alone, what's one thing I know for sure about Jesus?"

I'll demonstrate how asking the Oprah Question works in a moment, but first it's important to emphasize how this simple question can operate like a redemptive (red) stop sign in every area of our lives, not just when we're reading the words of Jesus in the New Testament. We can also ask the Oprah Question ("What's one thing I know for sure about Jesus?") whenever we're...

- reconciling the story of God in the Old and New Testaments;
- facing a tough decision;
- facing a choice between two good things;
- helping someone who's in crisis;
- considering popular teachings about Jesus;
- exploring ways to tell others about Jesus;
- tackling questions about what Jesus said and did;
- praying for others or for yourself; and
- responding to popular criticisms of Christianity.

The more we ask the Oprah Question, the more it grows into a natural and repetitive habit in all the circumstances of life. You won't need to remember to ask, because not asking will seem strange. The elegant simplicity of "What's one thing you know for sure about Jesus?" masks its clear leverage—there are many things we think we know about Jesus, but what do we know *for sure*? It's the *for sure* that makes this a transformative question.

As a random exercise in asking the Oprah Question, here's an experiment. Choose one chapter from Matthew's Gospel that's loaded with red stuff— chapter 15 works well. Then quickly determine what you know *for sure* about Jesus as you scan through the things he said and did (if your Bible doesn't have red letters, just pay attention to places where Jesus speaks). Since we're focusing on an entire chapter, don't confine yourself to only one thing you know for sure about Jesus—just keep answering the question every time you encounter something he said or did. This shouldn't take long—you're moving quickly through the red stuff and scribbling notes as you move. Even though you're scanning, not digging, you will need to consider the question well: "What's one thing I know for sure about Jesus here and here and here?" Now is a good time to stop and try this. I'll do the same, and then you can compare what you discovered to my list...

(Cue the elevator music.)

Okay, here's how I answered the Oprah Question as I read through Matthew 15...

- Jesus likes to answer questions with questions, especially in confrontational situations.
- Jesus is not afraid to speak truth to power.

• Jesus is intent on smoking out hypocrisy whenever he smells the stink of it.

• Jesus uses Scripture as an anchor in contentious conversations.

• Jesus knows Scripture well enough to cite it in relevant circumstances.

• Jesus is more interested in the spirit of the Law than the letter of the Law.

• Jesus is less interested in the words we use to represent who we are than the actions that reveal who we really are.

• Jesus decries the outward focus people give to maintaining a righteous exterior, and he challenges them to consider what comes out of them more than what goes into them.

• Jesus is determined to expose and dismantle untruth wherever he finds it.

• Jesus knows that all truth emanates from God alone.

• Jesus is brutally choosy about the people we follow or allow to influence us.

• Jesus uses metaphor all the time to help us understand kingdom-of-God truth.

• Jesus is not shy about confronting lazy thinking.

• Jesus has a good working knowledge of our biology and how it mirrors our spiritual patterns.

• Jesus often withdrew from the crowds so he could re-center himself.

• Jesus is not driven by sympathy—he's intent on loving us, not sympathizing with us.

• Jesus is wildly unpredictable.

• Jesus is not afraid to offend people.

• Jesus can be surprised and astonished by our acts of faith and persistence.

• Jesus heals people—lots and lots of people.

• Jesus is never daunted by the needs we bring to him—nothing seems impossible to him.

• Jesus is intent on revealing the great love God has for his children.

• Jesus is aware of our physical needs and feels compassion for them.

• Jesus does not let physical limitations keep him from meeting needs.

• Jesus is extravagantly generous.

"At the beginning of my life of following Jesus, he gave me two verses to hold in my hand and heart for life. These always help me come back to 'true north.' They remind me of what I want when I'm my true self with him, and they remind me of what he wants and his desire for me. They are Matthew 6:33 ('Seek the Kingdom of God above all else, and live righteously, and he will give you everything you need') and 2 Corinthians 11:3 ('But I fear that somehow your pure and undivided devotion to Christ will be corrupted, just as Eve was deceived by the cunning ways of the serpent')." —Bob Krulish

Now, after this short exercise, get in touch with your own worship level—I know I'm more deeply affected by the breadth and depth of who Jesus is right now, and I can't help myself from wanting to revel in him. "Betcha can't eat just one" has been the Lays potato chip slogan for 50 years, but it also describes our taste of Jesus. Whenever we focus on the red stuff by asking the Oprah Question, this is the fruit that's produced. We're drawn like magnets to him, and we give our soul something solid to feed on. Because we're simply letting the scriptural accounts speak to us about Jesus, we're edging our way closer to "all-in" with him, all the time. This simple playground practice—asking the Oprah Question about the red stuff—will transform the way you relate to him, especially when you're wallowing in mud puddles with him.

Endnotes

1 Louis Klopsch, "Explanatory Note," in *The Holy Bible: Red Letter Edition* (New York, NY: Christian Herald, 1901), xvi.

—12—

Remembering, Not Imagining

"The moon reflects the sun's light. We can relax—if we'll just keep junk from floating in between us and the sun, our light will shine..."

—Tom Melton

A well-known church consultant was talking about cultural trends that are having an impact on the church today. I heard lots of facts and illustrations about "top down" versus "bottom up," "dictatorial" versus "participatory," "isolating" versus "connecting," "big box" versus "intimate space," and so on. She used her words like a surgeon would use a scalpel—cutting open the patient (the church) to first expose what was killing her and then removing what needed to go. I knew her scalpel skills were impressive, but something about the operation left me dissonant.

I realized the church consultant was only exploring horizontal strategies—I mean, plans and ideas and techniques that promise to improve our experience of church and Christian fellowship. Metaphorically, it was a very, very interesting discussion about the cup-holders in a Ferrari—but who cares about the accessories when you have 500 horsepower sitting under the hood? Even though Jesus is the most fascinating and significant person of all time (even the editors of *Time Magazine* agree), almost all the very interesting discussions and movements in the church are about cup-holders—techniques and philosophies and approaches that excite because they are new or edgy or hip.

And, I must say, they are *incredibly boring* when they're placed side-by-side with the unadulterated person of Jesus.

I raised my hand to ask the church consultant: "I'd like to throw out to you my own little 'axe to grind' and get your response. Everything you're talking about is very interesting but very horizontal to me...so where does the pursuit of Jesus fit into all of this?" The consultant looked at me for an uncomfortably long moment—my question was a dangerous rabbit-trail that threatened to distract her attention from the patient she was working so hard to save. "Well, of course, we can't forget the story in all of this," the consultant said, finally. "In the midst of changing and adapting our ministries to meet the challenges of a rapidly changing culture, we have to hang on to what we've always known." The consultant continued down this path for another minute or two, and then was clearly ready to move on.

I think we're now at a place where we're so comfortable with Jesus, so confident of who he is and what he's like, that a lot of 'what we know' is actually *wrong*.

So I did something you're not supposed to do when you've already raised your hand once—I raised it again. To her credit, she stopped to acknowledge my interruption. And then I offered my mid-marriage malaise analogy to her: "Actually, I don't think it's a good idea at all to 'hang on to what we know'—I think we're now at a place where we're so comfortable with Jesus, so confident of who he is and what he's like, that a lot of 'what we know' is actually *wrong*. We've kind of lost interest in him, like a married couple in midlife. We think we pretty much have him pegged—all the things we like and all the things that have been bugging us about him for years. We've been married a long time to Jesus and have gone through a lot together. But one of the marriage partners, the church, is sort of looking around for something to spark our passions because we're past the 'passionate curiosity' stage with Jesus. So we turn to the 'form and function' of doing church as a kind of midlife splurge—like letting ourselves get involved in an emotional affair to rouse us from our relational boredom. If we're not awake to this dynamic, our 'marriage' could descend into deadness and a sense of growing isolation; we'll literally live under the same roof with Jesus but live separate lives, functionally apart from him."

"What all people are *really* hungry for today is Jesus."

Of course, this diatribe took way too long to spew, and I was almost immediately self-conscious about it. I felt like a pressure-cooker letting off steam. The woman exercised remarkable patience with me—when I was finished fire-hosing her, she nodded, acknowledged my input, and abruptly suggested we take a short break. I got up to stretch and was shocked when I was quickly surrounded by a small throng. Were they about to complain about my arrogance or argue about my premise? Well, as it turned out, no... Their eyes were flashing with a kind of rebel glee, and they were smiling. One of them said, leaning in with excitement, "What all people are *really* hungry for today is Jesus." The others quickly nodded. Our faces lit up and we felt an immediate and kindred closeness with each other. The excitement of our shared passion for Jesus was, simply, a non-musical expression of worship.

"I receive the body and blood of Jesus, partaking in the mysterious meal he offers. Something happens at the table—Jesus comes close and feeds me in ways beyond words. But I know I've been fed, and I keep coming back to his table." —Kelley Nikondeha

It's true that a steady diet of Jesus-lite has made us ravenous for a Jesus-feast. But we don't want to *imagine* what it would be like to eat and drink Jesus in a "What would Jesus do?" scenario. We want a Jesus who will fill the hole in our soul—the real Jesus we've never really explored very deeply. We need to remember this Jesus, not imagine a Jesus that doesn't really exist. And so we focus on the things we *know* Jesus did, rather than take wild guesses about what he'd do if he were in our present circumstances. We anchor our relationship with him in reality.

> "I focus on what I receive *in* Jesus, and not on what I achieve *for* Jesus." —Derwin Gray

Remembering Jesus simply means living in the spirit of Lombardi—returning to the stories about him that we thought we already had dialed-in and tasting them with a fresh palate. For example...

• The Woman at the Well (John 4:1-30)—What if the point of Jesus' interaction with this woman was to surface her shame so she could be freed from it? And what if he has the same intentions with us?

• The Healing of the Man by the Pool of Bethesda (John 5:1-15)—What if the point of Jesus' interaction with this crippled man, lying incapacitated by this infamous pool in Jerusalem for 38 years, was to challenge him to ask for what he really wanted? And what if he has the same intentions with us?

• The Healing of the Man Born Blind (John 9:1-7)—What if the point of Jesus' interaction with this blind man, when he smears mud on the man's face and tells him to somehow find his way to the distant Pool of Siloam so he can be healed, is to gauge how much the man is willing to risk? And what if he has the same intentions with us?

And as we do the things Jesus did, depending on his Spirit for the strength and courage to do them, we understand his heart more deeply.

When we remember to remember Jesus—to re-approach him with childlike curiosity over and over—we are also slowly learning to live under the influence of his sensibilities. We end up doing the things that Jesus did, worshipping him through the gracious work of radical hospitality. And as we do the things Jesus did, depending on his Spirit for the strength and courage to do them, we understand his heart more deeply. There's a deep connection here—we come to know him more intimately as we say and do the things he says and does. In *Mere Christianity*, C.S. Lewis writes:

> We have to be continually reminded of what we believe. Neither this belief nor any other will automatically remain alive in the mind. It must be fed. And as a matter of fact, if you examined a hundred people who had lost their faith in Christianity, I wonder how many of them would turn out to have been reasoned out of it by honest argument? Do not most people simply drift away?[1]

In our conventional approaches to life, we are like little children building a Soapbox Derby car out of plywood for a Formula One race when there's a perfectly good Ferrari sitting there. God is not expecting us to create our own car, building it out of scrap wood and ingenuity—he's inviting us to sink into the bucket seats of his Ferrari, whose name is Jesus, and open up the throttle. So we come back again and again to the stories and teachings of Jesus, with the assumption that we've forgotten what is most important about them. And then we consider the implications of our fresh taste by finding ways to live it out.

What would it look like for me, today, to finally ask Jesus for what I really want?

Or to confess to him what I am ashamed to admit to others?

Or to take a risk in a close relationship, for the sake of the other's freedom?

We ask the Spirit to give us a nudge, and then we respond by acting on the nudge. This is living the Lombardi life, where remembering is far more important to us than imagining.

Endnotes

1 C.S. Lewis, *Mere Christianity* (New York, NY: HarperSanFrancisco, 2015), 142.

—13—

☑ DO
☒ DON'T
☑ DO

Noticing What Jesus Did & Didn't Do

"I read the Bible often, I try to read it right. As far as I can understand, it's nothing but a burning light."

—Bruce Cockburn

Dr. Amy-Jill Levine has a passion for Jesus. In fact, she's spent her entire professional career studying him, working with other academics who, she says, "also find him fascinating and inspirational." She is a leading expert in the world on the person and practice of Jesus, writing highly acclaimed books about him. And that's why her official Vanderbilt Divinity School bio is a bit of a surprise: "Yankee Jewish feminist who teaches in a predominantly Christian divinity school in the buckle of the Bible Belt."

Wait. What?

Yes, Levine remains a Jew who says she does *not* worship Jesus as God, but can't stop thinking about him all the time. She is ruined by Jesus and ruined for Jesus. But she somehow can't cross the bridge from empirical respect to heart worship. She tried to explain this dichotomy to Christian journalist Jonathan Merritt,[1] who interviewed her shortly after the release of her bestselling work of historical criticism, *Short Stories by Jesus: The Enigmatic Parables of a Controversial Rabbi.*

People who think of me as a misfit because I do not worship Jesus are operating under a category confusion. Faith is not based in logic; faith is not derived from empirical observation or historical data (see here 1 Corinthians 1:23)—it comes from the heart, not the head. Belief is not like Sudoku; it is like love.

Levine is saying that Jesus has conquered her head, but not her heart. From personal experience, I know it's difficult to resist the gravitational pull of Jesus when you get this close to him, so maybe Levine so deeply identifies herself as a Jew and a feminist and an academic that it's just too hard for her to admit what's already true deep below the surface of her soul. Her fascination with Jesus may have long since morphed into worship down there, but it would be culturally and academically problematic for her to admit it. Or we take her at her word and recognize that she must be continually firing her rocket-thrusters to ensure her orbit maintains a safe distance from him. In any case, Levine believes that most Western Christians have missed the magnetic truth about Jesus because they don't really understand the things he did and didn't do. For example:

• Jesus radically changed the way people see God, teaching things about him that had never been taught before. Levine says:

Jesus is the first person in literature called "rabbi," which at the time—the late first century—meant "teacher"... To see Jesus as a rabbi, a Jewish teacher, is to take seriously what he had to say: his parables, interpretation of the Scriptures of Israel, apocalyptic pronouncements, ethical guides—and all of these teachings can only be fully appreciated if we see how they fit into their own historical context.

• Jesus told parables—stories that served as a hook for his time-bomb truths—as a primary teaching strategy. But Levine says our contemporary reactions to these parables are skewed:

We do not hear the parables the way Jesus' initial audiences would have heard them. First, we miss the allusions those first hearers would have recognized. Second, we are heirs to two millennia of Christian interpretation—interpretations already begun by the Evangelists. Third, we miscue the genre: today parables are often seen as children's stories, as statements of the obvious, or as designed to comfort. That original audience knew that parables were challenges, or even indictments. Finally, we often miss the humor. By domesticating the parables and ignoring their challenge, we lose their provocation, and their punch.

Levine is leaning into Jesus with peculiar attention to the things he said and did. And this is also how we unlock his essence and beauty. This is so easy to do that it doesn't take *any* academic training to develop the same filter in our lives. We can all practice a simple habit I call "Jesus Did/Jesus Didn't." Here's a taste of how this works. (You'll need something to write with and access to a print or digital Bible.) Below you'll see two columns: "Jesus Did" and "Jesus Didn't." The idea is to choose a passage from one of the four Gospels—Matthew, Mark, Luke, or John—and write things that Jesus did in that passage on the left; then write things he didn't do on the right. Simply read through the passage you've chosen, looking for things Jesus embraced, advised, or did, and list them under the "Jesus Did" column. Then, to spark your thinking even more, go back through that list and brainstorm the opposite of each thing you've listed. For example, if you write, "He healed people of sickness" on the "Jesus Did" side, you can write, "He didn't ignore or leave sick those who came to him seeking healing."

Let's give this practice a spin by focusing on John 6. You do your own short list, and then you can turn the page to see what I did with it...

(Elevator music.)

JESUS DID	JESUS DIDN'T

JESUS DID	JESUS DIDN'T
• Jesus is proactive about choosing when to be with crowds and when to retreat with his friends.	• Jesus doesn't let others determine what he needs.
• Jesus tests our faith to see how we react to challenges.	• Jesus doesn't always make it easy to follow him.
• Jesus gets personally involved in meeting our needs, both spiritual and physical.	• Jesus doesn't outsource meeting needs to others.
• Jesus made sure that food was not wasted.	• Jesus doesn't treat resources as things to simply throw away.
• Jesus will not be used by people who have ulterior motives.	• Jesus doesn't suffer fools.
• Jesus regularly spends time alone.	• Jesus doesn't need to be around others all the time.
• Jesus is comfortable acting supernaturally—he exercises his authority over every natural law.	• Jesus doesn't make a big difference between natural and supernatural.
• Jesus will both scare us and comfort us.	• Jesus doesn't always calm all our fears—he actually instigates some of them.
• Jesus understands the hidden motivations of the people around him, and he drags it all into the light.	• Jesus doesn't ignore the games we try to play with him—he exposes them.
• Jesus insists that we believe in him and will not offer ironclad evidence to convince us.	• Jesus doesn't answer all our questions or remove all our doubts.
• Jesus offers us what we really need—he does not settle for merely what we think we need.	• Jesus doesn't let himself be swayed by arguments that don't mesh with his will.
• Jesus does not always explain himself or his teaching—he forces us to wrestle with it first.	• Jesus doesn't mind making us uncomfortable.
• Jesus wants a shockingly intimate relationship with us.	• Jesus does not want to be our buddy—he wants to be our Lover.
• Jesus defers to his Father's will, not his own.	• Jesus does not act arrogantly.
• Jesus will say and do things that throw us into dissonance.	• Jesus is not intent on making things easy for us.
• Jesus is comfortable leaving people to wrestle with their doubts.	• Jesus does not adjust what he says and does to make himself more palatable.
• Jesus is open, honest, and vulnerable.	• Jesus does not keep people at a distance.
• Jesus is relaxed around evil—he is not afraid to engage it.	• Jesus does not react with fear over the threat of evil.

Just as the Oprah Question ("What's one thing I know for sure about Jesus, based only on this passage?") can infiltrate our thinking so deeply that it becomes like breathing to us, this Jesus Did/Jesus Didn't mentality can grow into a reflexive practice. Whether you use it on a broader scale (as a specific filter when you're reading or studying the Bible) or in a micro way (pausing to ask, "What did Jesus really do here?" and "What didn't Jesus do here?" whenever you're focusing your attention on him), it has real traction when it becomes a way of life, not a mere strategy. And if you actually did this little exercise just now, my guess is that if you do it just one more time your brain will learn to ride this bike for the rest of your life—you won't be able to stop reading the Bible this way, whether or not you actually write anything down.

The Jesus Did/Jesus Didn't mentality both deconstructs and reconstructs the truth about him.

"In addition to readings that have been part of my morning time with Jesus, I've added an element this year that came out of my conviction about Jesus' last instructions to his disciples in Acts 1. Basically, he told them to wait for the Holy Spirit. The remainder of Acts 1 then chronicles what they did after he ascended and left them. Assuming they needed to replace Judas, they went to work casting lots, and selected Matthias. The selecting of Matthias doesn't seem to disqualify them from God's purposes, but neither does it produce anything, as we never hear of Matthias again. Seems to be more like 'wood, hay, and stubble' versus 'gold, silver, or precious stones.' It got me thinking: *How much of my life is about replacing Matthiases versus waiting for the Holy Spirit?*" —Scott Larson

The Jesus Did/Jesus Didn't mentality both deconstructs and reconstructs the truth about him. For example, here's what happened when I searched for "Jesus healed" on BibleGateway.com—in this sampler, notice what Jesus says and does, and doesn't say and do, around each healing or demon ejection (all quotations are from NIV):

• Matthew 9:22—"Jesus turned and saw her. 'Take heart, daughter,' he said, 'your faith has healed you.' And the woman was healed at that moment."

• Matthew 12:22—"Then they brought him a demon-possessed man who was blind and mute, and Jesus healed him, so that he could both talk and see."

• Matthew 15:28—"Then Jesus answered, 'Woman, you have great faith! Your request is granted.' And her daughter was healed at that moment."

• Mark 1:34—"And Jesus healed many who had various diseases. He also drove out many demons, but he would not let the demons speak because they knew who he was."

• Luke 9:42—"Even while the boy was coming, the demon threw him to the ground in a convulsion. But Jesus rebuked the evil spirit, healed the boy and gave him back to his father."

• John 5:13—"The man who was healed had no idea who it was, for Jesus had slipped away into the crowd that was there."

Notice how Jesus healed people—cared for their most desperate, temporal needs—without the kind of deal-closing behavior we look for to legitimize service-oriented outreach. I mean, he didn't require that people follow him or even believe in him before he healed them. This means that when we love people by helping them with no strings attached, we're moving in the Spirit of Jesus and we're exercising radical hospitality. We discover this by considering what he did do, and what he *didn't* do, when he healed people.

Jesus never modeled or advocated maintaining a distance from his culture.

You can make the same observation about the way we engage our wider culture. Jesus never modeled or advocated maintaining a distance from his culture. In fact, he so closely attached himself to "worldly" people and environments that some claimed he was "of the world" himself. If we think we're maturing in our relationship with Jesus by repeatedly damning popular music, contemporary books, and current movies and video games, we're confused. We can't hide from the culture we live in, or simply blast its most obviously pagan aspects. If we do, we either adopt a survival mentality that fuels rigid, powerless, and self-centered living over impacting the world with the truth Jesus died defending, or we develop two alter egos so they can function in both the mainstream world and the church world. Relative to cultural influences, Jesus either celebrated them or subverted them—but he *didn't* cloister himself from them.

"In our culture, there's a movement away from simple love songs to Jesus. But not for me...I listen to worship music—nothing cool and exotic like Gregorian chant. I like contemporary music from Bethel, Hillsong, Vineyard, David Crowder, Sanctus Real, and so on. I wake up to it and sometimes go to sleep to it. These songs quiet my heart and still my soul in a way that connects me to Jesus like nothing else." —Carl Medearis

When we focus on the red stuff and deeply consider the things Jesus did and didn't do, we anchor our faith in the reality of who he is, not in conjecture.

Endnotes

1 Quotes are from "Seeing the Gospel Through a Jewish Lens: An Interview With Amy-Jill Levine," by Jonathan Merritt, posted on the Religion News Service website on January 2, 2015.

—14—

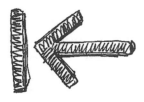

Practicing the Jesus Pushback

"Atheists really have a very strong presence now in the media, and claim that science has disproved the existence of God. I disagree with that. Science is a wonderful thing that teaches us a lot about the world. But what we learn requires so much extremely complex mathematics... How can we say that there's no God behind it?"

—Dr. Amir Aczel

I work out at an athletic club four times a week—a pattern I started years ago, when I tricked myself into losing 45 pounds. Sometimes I look around the weight room at all of the men and women pushing, pulling, and pumping, and I wonder what an alien would think if he/she saw what I saw. A hundred years ago, there was no market for athletic clubs and weight rooms because everyday life was so physically demanding for the average person. The dawn of the industrial revolution and the movement toward white-collar office jobs changed all that. For most people today, staying healthy means pursuing some kind of physical fitness regimen. That quadriceps machine I use every week is necessary because I'm not using my quads to lift hay bales onto a cart. I'm doing things that look, well, a little ridiculous, because I have to replace what I've lost—the strenuous physical activity of my ancestors' everyday lives. My artificial physical activities compensate for my sedentary life.

Yes, people in Western society have an obesity problem that must be addressed through diet and fitness. *But we have a much more subtle loss replacement need, and it's going to require a kind of mental fitness that's at least as important as our need for physical fitness.*

The "muscle" we need to strengthen more than any other is the one that fuels our critical thinking.

The "muscle" we need to strengthen more than any other is the one that fuels our critical thinking. I'm referring to our ability to push back against the lazy assumptions and partial truths about Jesus and the kingdom of God that we encounter almost every day. Read any popular book for Christians that was published 50 or 100 years ago (by C.S. Lewis or Malcolm Muggeridge or G.K. Chesterton or Dorothy Sayers, for example), and then compare that book to most of what is popular today—you'll quickly realize that the average reader in contemporary society has a flabby critical-thinking muscle compared to our grandparents and great-grandparents. Just as we have lost the physical challenges of everyday life that keep obesity at bay, we've lost the critical thinking expectations that keep us from obesity of the mind.

Lesslie Newbigin says: "What we call self-evident truths are not self-evident to me, and vice versa. When they speak of reason they mean what is reasonable within their plausibility structure."[1] (Again, "plausibility structures" are defined as "patterns of beliefs and practice accepted within a given society.") Newbigin goes on: "And when, in this culture, 'reason' is set against the specific, historically shaped tradition of Christian belief, it is obvious that what is happening is that the 'plausibility structure' is performing its normal function. The Christian, on the other hand, will relativize the reigning plausibility structure in the light of the gospel."[2] Newbigin is challenging followers of Jesus to love him with all their heart, soul—and *mind*. To push back against reigning plausibility structures—our accepted conventional truths that are actually a mix of truth and lie—by comparing them to the truths revealed and practiced by Jesus.

Pastor and author John Ortberg says:

In the Gospel of Mark, the scribes asked Jesus, "Which commandment is the most important of all?" And Jesus quotes from Deuteronomy 6:5—"You shall love the Lord your God with all your heart and with all your soul and with all your might"—but added the admonition to love God "with all your mind." Why the addition? Cornelius Plantinga called this the Magna Carta for the Christian intellectual life. To love God with all our minds means we...think about Him a lot.[3]

Whenever we encounter half-truths that are fueled by popular plausibility in our culture, we develop the mental muscle to spot them and counter them with the truth about Jesus and his kingdom.

Jesus himself did this all the time. I've already mentioned that he often used a formal critical-thinking rhythm to expose the plausibility structures that were popular in ancient Palestine: "You have heard it said that [fill in something that's passed off as the 'truth' in the culture], but I say [fill in a truth that Jesus reveals about the kingdom of God]." He's showing his followers how to push back against lazy thinking and silly beliefs. Contrary to popular assumptions, Jesus isn't an anti-intellectual. In fact, he's challenged us to maximize our minds in our pursuit of him, and in the way we live our lives for him. The practice I call "The Jesus Pushback" is a critical-thinking skill that will help us get inside the skin of Jesus—to think like he thinks about the influences that are exerting leverage on us. In it, we simply use the framework Jesus has already given us ("You have heard it said..., but I say...") to compare and contrast the common beliefs and conventional wisdoms of our culture. To start, we drag commonly accepted "truths" in our culture into the light and then match them with a kingdom-of-God truth that Jesus revealed.

Let's give this a try with a few sampler "truths" that match up well with what Jesus taught in Matthew 5, commonly called The Beatitudes...

YOU HAVE HEARD IT SAID...	BUT I SAY...
• The weak and unsuccessful in life are modern-day lepers—they are not people we want to hang around.	• "Blessed are the poor in spirit, for theirs is the kingdom of heaven."
• Never let them see you cry.	• "Blessed are those who mourn, for they shall be comforted."
• If you want to succeed in life, you'll need to push your way to the top.	• "Blessed are the gentle, for they shall inherit the earth."
• Do whatever makes you happy and you'll find fulfillment.	• "Blessed are those who hunger and thirst for righteousness, for they shall be satisfied."
• The only way people will respect you is if they know they'll get hurt if they mess with you.	• "Blessed are the merciful, for they shall receive mercy."
• People who shelter themselves from the broad range of cultural influences are missing out.	• "Blessed are the pure in heart, for they shall see God."
• The goal is to win, not to make friends.	• "Blessed are the peacemakers, for they shall be called sons of God."
• At all costs, bite your lip when someone says something that's just not true—no one will want to hang out with you if you're always spouting that "religious" stuff.	• "Blessed are those who have been persecuted for the sake of righteousness, for theirs is the kingdom of heaven."
• The worst thing in the world is to be the target of false rumors and accusations.	• "Blessed are you when people insult you and persecute you, and falsely say all kinds of evil against you because of Me. Rejoice and be glad, for your reward in heaven is great; for in the same way they persecuted the prophets who were before you."

When we practice this "You have heard it said…, but I say…" rhythm often enough, we turn on that switch that can't be turned off—ever. We learn to think through a permanent filter. It's called holy skepticism—when we're operating in it, we accept no conventional truths that contradict the truths Jesus revealed. We learn to think like him in every circumstance because we're discovering how countercultural he was in his thinking.

"I journal. Writing my thoughts, my prayers, and my questions—all the way out to the end of the sentence—helps me articulate my place in things. And as I write, I create a space where I often hear Jesus respond between the lines somehow. We meet in the words scribbled across pages." —Kelley Nikondeha

I guarantee you'll ram into a culturally accepted plausibility structure today—whether in conversation, in the media, or on social media. For example:

• People who are "good enough" will end up going to heaven when they die (but Jesus tells us he's the only way into eternal life).

• The best way to please God is to keep all of his rules (but Jesus tells us to "eat My flesh and drink My blood" if we want to make him happy).

• People who say they have conversations with God are more or less insane (but Jesus tells us the Spirit's job description is to fuel an ongoing, conversational relationship with us).

• Jesus is basically a nice guy and a good teacher who wouldn't hurt a fly (but Jesus is actually more ferocious than nice, and he often "hurt" the people around him because he was more in interested in their redemption than their comfort).

• If you're a churchgoing person, you're probably a "holier than thou" hypocrite (but Jesus said, "I have come to call not those who think they are righteous, but those who know they are sinners and need to repent").

The more we have embedded in our minds the words of Jesus ("You have heard it said..."), the more alert we will be to the accepted half-truths of our contemporary culture.

The more we have embedded in our minds the words of Jesus ("You have heard it said..."), the more alert we will be to the accepted half-truths of our contemporary culture. Learn to think in a Jesus Pushback way by simply noticing whenever you hear a "given," and ask yourself what Jesus would say back to that "given." You won't have to brainstorm what he might say, because you have the Spirit of Jesus within you. Ask him about his response to that "given," and then listen and learn. You can also, of course, compare any "givens" you hear to what you find Jesus has already said or done in the scriptural account of his life, or throw it out there to your community of Jesus-followers to gauge its broad acceptance.

"I pass on what I am learning to a handful of brothers and sisters. I learn and grow and become excited about my faith the more I teach. Psychologists call this 'the protégé effect,' and I am a clear example of this. So when I place myself within this stream of discipleship, where I am being discipled as well as discipling others, I come more fully alive to Jesus." —Bruxy Cavey

Endnotes

1 Newbigin, *The Gospel in a Pluralist Society*, 65.

2 Ibid, 57.

3 John Ortberg, *Who Is This Man?* (Grand Rapids, MI: Zondervan, 2014), 63.

Redefining Truth

"Jesus is The Truth. We believe in Him—not merely in His words. He is…the Revealer and the Revelation, the Illuminator and the Light of Men. He is exalted in every word of truth, because he is its sum and substance… A Christless gospel is no gospel at all and a Christless discourse is the cause of merriment to devils."

—Charles Haddon Spurgeon

Jesus doesn't merely point the way to true things, or give us an example of what is true; *he is Truth itself.* So, the best way to know Jesus more intimately is to look at him through this filter: Whatever he says and does is the very definition of truth, because Jesus is the source of everything that is true. Chasing the people selling "God-junk" out of the Temple with a whip he created on the spot? Truth. Calling the religious power brokers of his day, the Pharisees, offensive names like "whitewashed tombs" and "brood of vipers"? Truth. Praising a sinful woman who crashed a society party and washed his feet with her tears? Truth. No matter what he says or does, the source of his behavior is truth.

Our culture immerses us in false things that pass themselves off as true things.

The more we slow down to consider how Jesus embodies truth, the more we attach ourselves to the Vine, and the less likely we are to mistake "false" for "true." And that's crucial, because our culture immerses us in false things that pass themselves off as true things. A closer relationship with Truth makes us hyper-aware of the falsehoods that insinuate themselves into our lives, exposing what is holding us back from offering the full impact of who we are.

> "I intentionally teach or lead by exercising discernment—my gifts are optimized when I'm on full alert to Jesus' promptings." —Dave Rahn

For example, what are you afraid of? Stop to consider the question and you'll likely discover a longer list than you assumed. Fear is our most powerful human emotion, deeply rooted in our ability to survive as humans. Fear helps us discern threats to our physical or psychological health and either resist them or flee from them. Our "fight or flight" response is a species survival mechanism. But that explanation doesn't really unravel, on the face of it, why so many of us (1 in 10) fear clowns—the eradication of clowns will not likely improve our percentage chances of surviving as a species. And our false fear of clowns is just one ridiculous example of a non-ridiculous human condition—most of us live as captives to fear, imprisoned in false cells with imaginary bars.

Since Jesus is the Truth, he's also the chief practitioner of "exposure therapy" in our lives— he not only exposes our fears, he often *causes* them, because Truth will not coexist with false.

Fear properly calibrated to actual risks is a crucial necessity for life. Fear that overextends itself or even fabricates risk is a harmful and destructive force, stealing from us the freedom Jesus came to give us. And how do we overcome these life-stealing falsehoods? Well, scientists and psychologists agree that the most effective method is something called "exposure therapy"—it requires us to repeatedly confront our fears, which helps us suppress the memory or the environmental trigger that hooks us into the cycle. The more we confront the truth about the fears that surround us, the less likely we are to be at their mercy. This is why confronting the brutal facts of your reality (remember the Stockdale Paradox?) is so crucial to overcoming our fears. Since Jesus is the Truth, he's also the chief practitioner of exposure therapy in our lives—he not only exposes our fears, he often *causes* them, because Truth will not coexist with false.

For example, after Jesus feeds more than 5,000 people on a remote hillside, a frenzied mob intends to forcibly install him as king. So he withdraws to the wilderness to be by himself. His disciples wait for him by the shores of the Sea of Galilee for hours, but it's getting dark. So they get in their boat without Jesus to cross over to Capernaum. They've rowed into the dark, and into the teeth of a gathering storm, when they encounter the most frightening thing any of them have ever seen: Out of the gloom comes Jesus, walking on the water toward them. Their first, terrified thought is that it must be a ghost heading toward them—trapped in a boat in the middle of the sea on a stormy night.

Of course, Jesus understands what a man might feel if he sees a person walking on the sea in the middle of a storm in the middle of the night. He is *intending* to provoke their fears. He is using exposure therapy to help them confront a false fear (ghosts) and summon the courage to overcome it with the truth. So he identifies himself and asks his disciples to let him in the boat—to believe in who he is. And they do. John understates the tipping point: "So they were willing to receive Him into the boat" (John 6:21). "Willing to receive" means they had to choose to move into and through their fears. They are learning, through their exposure to the Truth, to properly slot their false fears under their overarching commitment to Jesus. How many ghosts have you invited into your boat? Jesus will root out every false thing in our lives and replace it with a deeper appreciation for, and trust in, the Truth.

"Jesus invites me to face what's true and feel what's true—he meets me in the moment with his transcendent goodness." —Steve Merritt

Truth always matters, in every situation. In a two-hour training I do called "Fighting the Entitlement Dragon," I ask parents if it's more likely that their kids would get abducted by a stranger or hit by lightning. It's always no contest—FAR more parents believe their kids are at greater risk of being kidnapped by a stranger. But the facts say their kids have TWICE the chance of getting hit by lightning than being abducted by a stranger. When we live with false fears and false beliefs, we waste our strength on futile safeguards and ineffective formulas—our thoughts are gripped by false anxieties. Jesus intends to help us reject the influence of false so that we can live in Truth. And the more we taste the Truth, the less we like the taste of false. Edwin Friedman pinpoints the underlying reason our culture seems stuck in a swirl of ineffective leadership—because of our false fears, he says, *we have valued safety over adventure.* "[Contemporary] civilization," he writes, "influences our thoughts and our leaders toward safety and certainty vs. boldness and adventure."[1]

Jesus intends to help us reject the influence of false so that we can live in Truth.

When we abide in the One whose name is Truth, we're less likely to stay locked behind our imaginary cell bars. As Tonio K reminds us, *"When we get sprung from out these cages, baby, God knows what we might do."* And so the Spirit of Truth creates a love for truth in all its forms, and spurs us to question cultural truths and conventional wisdom and prevalent plausibility structures. We ask questions like these:

• *Is it true in light of what I know about Jesus?* (Is that the way Jesus would really talk or act? Can you imagine Jesus urging people to get on board with it?)

• *Is it a truth embraced by the whole body of Christ?* (Jesus insists on a diversity of gifts and perspectives in his "Body"—so how would a "foot" experience this truth differently from a "hand"?)

• *Is it true in its biblical context?* (Has this truth been plucked out of its home in Scripture and treated like a sound bite?)

• *Is it true within the boundaries of things Jesus actually said and did?* (Our answer to "What would Jesus do?" is irrelevant if it doesn't have a natural connection to "What did Jesus do?")

• *Is it true based on what I already know is true about Jesus and the kingdom of God?* (Jesus told parables to help us understand how things work in the kingdom of God, so does this truth fit with what his parables have already revealed, or would it violate something Jesus has already made clear?)

• *Is it true on the face of it?* (If you scratch the surface of this truth, asking yourself if there's a solid foundation under the veneer, how quickly does it fall apart?)

• *Is the foundation or source of the information true, or has it been distorted somehow?* (Is this truth obviously serving a pre-determined agenda?)

• *Is it the full truth, or does it represent only disconnected snippets of truth?* (What has been left out, accidentally or on purpose, in the description or context of this truth?)

• *Is it a culturally bent truth that serves a self-centered agenda?* (Is it a truth that makes sense no matter where you live, or has it been reconfigured to support a narrow cultural perspective?)

When we study Jesus through the filter of truth, we quickly find him unmasking falsehood and redefining what's true, left and right.

Endnotes

1 Edwin Friedman, *A Failure of Nerve* (New York, NY: Seabury Books, 2007), 33.

Redefining Love

"God is the best enemy to have, because he's trying to save His enemies."

—Shane Farmer

Leonardo da Vinci was preparing to paint his masterpiece *The Last Supper*. On the eve of launching into this massive creative project, he and a fellow painter had a conflict that quickly descended into an angry, painful, and noisy fight. In the grip of his rage, da Vinci decided to use the face of this man as his model for the face of Judas Iscariot in his painting. This would be his revenge on his enemy, a subtle but accusing finger pointed at him for eternity. When people dropped in to see how da Vinci was progressing with his painting, he took great pleasure when they noticed the resemblance of Judas to his enemy. He continued his work until it was time to paint the face of Jesus. And then he got stuck. No matter how hard he tried to bring Jesus to life on his canvas, something wasn't working.

After repeated failures, it dawned on da Vinci that the hatred he savored for his fellow painter had become a huge blockage in his work, preventing him from finishing. He decided the only way to unblock his creative imagination was to remove the face of his enemy from the painting and create a different face for Judas. Once he had done this, he felt suddenly free to paint Jesus' face and complete one of the greatest works of art ever created.[1]

G.K. Chesterton tells us we'll have to redefine the way we describe love once we get to know Jesus more intimately, because Jesus loves in ways that are "beyond category" (Duke Ellington's phrase, used to describe a truly great jazz musician). A lot of people were uncomfortable in Jesus' presence and scandalized by things he said and did. Chesterton says it's hard to stand Jesus if we're really paying close attention to him, and if we persist in holding on to our conventional definitions of love. He's the most disruptive person who ever walked the earth. And he is so much better than our typical descriptions of him—so much more than a dispenser of life lessons or a teller of cute fables. He's the greatest lover the world has ever known—and his standard for love, as da Vinci discovered by accident, goes way beyond our categories:

You have heard the law that says, "Love your neighbor" and hate your enemy. But I say, love your enemies! Pray for those who persecute you! In that way, you will be acting as true children of your Father in heaven. For he gives his sunlight to both the evil and the good, and he sends rain on the just and the unjust alike. If you love only those who love you, what reward is there for that? Even corrupt tax collectors do that much. If you are kind only to your friends, how are you different from anyone else? Even pagans do that (Matthew 5:43-48, NLT).

Jesus asks an incriminating question here: If we love because we are loved, then how does that make us different from those who do not honor, worship, or carry the Spirit of Jesus in them? When we diminish the real Jesus, we also diminish our definition of love. That's why the leaders at Vintage Church in North Carolina decided to satirize the fake Jesus that many of us have come to know—to chip away at our wrong notions of Jesus so we can be reintroduced to the way he truly loves. They took a ridiculous and campy old film about Jesus, extracted four scenes from it, and recorded their own dialogue to replace the original audio. The result is hilarious (check out the videos on YouTube by searching for "Vintage Church Jesus Videos"). They give Jesus a falsetto Mr. Rogers' voice, making him the wimpy Jesus many people imagine. And they portray him as a distant rule-keeper who's out of touch with real life and severe in his interactions with his followers. The fake Jesus they're skewering offers a diminished, and diminishing, love to others—their satire is meant to stand in stark contrast to the enemy-loving Jesus who transforms lives.

When we diminish the real Jesus, we also diminish our definition of love.

Transformational love, not nicey-nice teddy bear love, is the only version we get with Jesus—a junior higher named Kenyon taught me that. I met Kenyon when I was 23. I was a counselor at Cross Bar X Youth Ranch, a Christian camp for low-income kids built on a plateau in the rugged southwestern mountains of Colorado. Because the teenagers at this camp often come from rough urban backgrounds, the camper-to-counselor ratio is low. That means that every day I spent almost all my waking hours with four guys who, in many ways, had way more life experience than me—but not the good kind of life experience.

"I cry out to Jesus when I feel lonely—sometimes I just need him to have skin on. When I do, I sense his loving and understanding smile. He assures me that he felt the same way about his Father, and that his Father smiled at him, too. This common rhythm—a cry followed by assurance—causes me to love Jesus even more." —Tom Melton

Kenyon had an enormous blond afro and a pair of fists that'd never met a face they didn't want to punch. He made up for his slight stature by adopting a junkyard-dog attitude. By the second day of camp, Kenyon had struck fear into the hearts of every other camper and (to be honest) most of the counselors. Out on the soccer field Kenyon had picked yet another fight. So I pulled him, flailing, from his latest victim and dragged him off the field. Discipline at Cross Bar X is simple—there's an 8-percent-grade, quarter-mile dirt road that shoots up the side of a plateau to the camp. When you step out of line at camp, your discipline is to run that hill from the bottom to the top—*with* the counselor who's disciplining you. So as

I dragged Kenyon toward the top of the road to walk down the hill, we rounded a bend and this little obscenity-spouting Tasmanian devil suddenly realized no one could see him anymore. To my shock, he just plopped down at the side of the road and started sobbing uncontrollably.

If he'd pulled a gun on me, I couldn't have been more taken off guard.

So I sat next to Kenyon in the dirt and put my arm around him. After a few minutes his sobbing tapered enough for me to ask him what was wrong. He looked up at me—the tears carving tracks down his dirty face—and cried out, "My parents don't love me!" I said, "Kenyon, of course they do—why do you think your parents don't love you?" "Because," he corrected me, "I can do anything, go anywhere, and hang out with anyone I want—they don't know and they don't care where I am or how soon I'll come home. I have no rules. I get whatever I want."

Because I was enforcing a boundary in Kenyon's life, he was feeling, for the first time, transformational love—a love that was not content to leave him as he was.

In a rush, I comprehended what was happening. Because I was enforcing a boundary in Kenyon's life, he was feeling, for the first time, transformational love—a love that was not content to leave him as he was. The love I was offering him was bent on remaking his heart, not ignoring it. And a little taste of beyond-category love struck a mother lode of grief inside his little-boy heart. That day I learned that kids who sense they should get whatever they want, whenever they want it, are really dying inside. They don't feel loved, because no one cares enough about them to be a catalyst for transformation in their lives.

Kenyon and I finally stood up and walked in silence down the hill. At the bottom I looked him in the eye, patted him on the back, and said, "Let's do this." We ran up that hill with a fury that the hope of transformation produces. Jesus is free to love us this way, with a determination to mold us, because he doesn't really *need* anything from us. All of his longings are focused on our release from captivity, not on the ways we can fulfill his unmet needs. And when we sink into him more deeply, his Spirit helps us begin to love those around us without *requiring* anything from them.

Jesus is looking for men and women who will respond to his intimate invitation to join him as he moves into the darkest places on earth on behalf of his troubled and besieged children. The Jesus-recipe for love mixes a hope that prevails with a determination to live clear-eyed in our brutal reality. And I taste that recipe in this story that a youth ministry friend shared with me:

We have a special-needs student who's pretty high-functioning. She kinda just hangs out by herself at youth group. But we have a really popular girl—she's the homecoming queen—who has befriended her. She picks this girl up and takes her out for pizza, and so on. This Sunday, as we wrapped up, the special-needs girl's mom came into our room to thank the other girl for befriending her daughter—she wanted to say that it meant a lot to both her and her daughter. The homecoming queen looked her dead in the eyes and said: "Why wouldn't I? She's an awesome girl and God loves her just as much as me." I lost it!

Here a high school homecoming queen is offering herself as a channel for the love of Jesus—a love that never lies about the brutal facts of our current reality, but also never stops believing that the beloved will prevail in the end. She's not making believe that the girl she's befriended is unaffected by her special needs, like so many would do to sidestep the obvious. She's loving her friend for who she is, not a romanticized version of her. The homecoming queen's "Why wouldn't I?" gently exposes the premise of the mother's "thank you"—that she's befriending her daughter, in some cloaked way, because she pities her. The girl's dead-in-the-eyes look says, instead: *There's no pity here—she's my friend because I think she's awesome.*

It is a love that invites others to discover the glorious truth about themselves, not settle for the inglorious lies they've unconsciously swallowed their whole lives.

"My upbringing was in a fundamentalist church that didn't put much stock in what I call "honest spirituality." I had to figure out on my own that my emotions counted, that Jesus cares how I feel about things. In learning to be honest with Jesus, I also discovered that my feelings are not a reliable basis for relationship. I discovered my emotions are essential to know the state of my heart, but like gauges on the dash of a car, they point to deeper issues. And it is those deeper issues that are the real stuff of intimacy with Jesus. So I tell Jesus how I feel—I use words to describe my hurts, reactions, disappointments, joys and achievements. But I also ask him to help me understand the deeper realities beneath my feelings. That's where the real intimacy happens—when my feelings connect to what Jesus sees and thinks, and his unchanging, rock-like character." —Floyd McClung

This is a love that transforms, not panders—and that is the way Jesus redefines love in those who love him. The Jesus-love we offer others is only "nice" when it needs to be—it is also fierce and exposing and uncomfortable when it needs to be. It is bent on offering others the seeds of transformation, not our passive permission to remain stagnant in a life that is self-destructing. It is a love that invites others to discover the glorious truth about themselves, not settle for the inglorious lies they've unconsciously swallowed their whole lives. The doorway into this kind of love is well-marked:

• It does not put a positive spin on the brutal realities of others—instead, it acknowledges those brutal realities as if they are weeds surrounding a flower. The flower is the person's intrinsic beauty, a characteristic that reflects something of the heart of Jesus. We see the weeds, but pay peculiar attention to the flower.

• It offers the *other* whatever it needs to move into greater life and freedom. For some, that means watering the plant with compassion, generosity, perseverance, and focused attention. For others, that means pruning branches that are choking the plant's growth. Watering is a lot less emotionally draining, compared to pruning. And pruning is risky, because you might cut something that you shouldn't. Pruning is a necessary aspect of Jesus' love flowing through us—but it is selective and restrained and aware that the plant will feel the pain of the cut.

• It gives not because the receiver deserves the gift, but because Jesus-love is transformational. The motivation for a love that's redefined by Jesus is grace—it is, by definition, undeserved.

• It is able to love enemies because it is not a transactional kind of love—"If you give, then I will give" or "If you deserve to be loved, then I will love you" or "If you treat me badly, then I will stop loving you." Instead, Jesus-love is a differentiated force. It loves because its source is the headwaters of Love, not because it has found the object of its love deserving.

The more time we spend hanging out inside the heart of Jesus, the more we are likely to be infected with his transformational way of loving. It invades us like a virus—life-giving rather than life-taking. We have to get close to people if we're going to be infected by whatever they have, so getting close to Jesus makes it possible for us to love the way he loves.

Endnotes

1 This story is attributed to "DaVinci," *The Mark Steel Lectures*. Series 2, Episode 2. The Open University. October 7, 2003. BBC.

17

Needing Him to Know Him

"[People] have more information about God than they have experiences of him. Get them in places where they have to rely on God."

—Tim Keller

I was driving Lucy, my 17-year-old daughter, home from youth group. She wanted to download some lingering questions from that night's small-group discussion. The leaders in her group targeted Paul's bold assertion that he'd "learned to be content in whatever circumstances" (Philippians 4:11). The girls in her group all agreed they were rarely content in *any* circumstance—always comparing themselves to others and worrying about their performance in school and in sports. The message Lucy took away from the discussion that followed was so typical of what I've said is the church's default advice on growing in Christ: *"Try harder to be better."*

Lucy and her friends left youth group that night thinking their way forward was to redouble their determination to fix the things that were wrong with them and recommit to overcoming sin in their lives. I squirmed in my seat and then said: "Lucy, that's not only a failed strategy, but it's not biblically true."

"What do you mean?" she asked. "I hear that answer all the time."

"I know," I said, "it's a form of growth-by-management that uniquely appeals to people living in Western culture, where 'pulling yourself up by your own bootstraps' is the 11th Commandment."

This mentality, I told her, is also what fuels our approach to sin. When we blow it, we vow to try harder the next time. And, as Dr. Phil likes to ask: "How's that working for you?" I'd bet a million dollars the honest answer is: "Not very well." Jesus, instead, urges us to abide in him so that the life that emanates from him will flow through us. Paul embraces this reality down to his toes. Let this ridiculously bold statement he makes in 1 Corinthians 4:1-4 (NLT) sink in:

So look at Apollos and me as mere servants of Christ who have been put in charge of explaining God's mysteries. Now, a person who is put in charge as a manager must be faithful. As for me, it matters very little how I might be evaluated by you or by any human authority. I don't even trust my own judgment on this point. My conscience is clear, but that doesn't prove I'm right. It is the Lord himself who will examine me and decide.

Wow. Paul is saying he *pays no attention* to whether or not he's done everything right in his stewardship of "God's mysteries"—he depends on the Spirit of God to let him know if he is. Why waste time managing yourself when a close, dependent relationship with Jesus will lead to a life that's marked by the Spirit's nudges—acquittal and conviction come from Jesus, not our own clouded perspective.

Paul is saying he *pays no attention* to whether or not he's done everything right in his stewardship of "God's mysteries"—he depends on the Spirit of God to let him know if he is.

This Jesus-dependent way of living has an incredible side effect: The more we depend on him, the deeper we come to know him. *To know him, we must need him.* Paul is offering clear evidence of his commitment to a dependent relationship with Jesus, not a self-dependent life. He's living his life with a "Ryder Box" embedded in his soul...

In 2007, the Ryder rental truck company launched something they called "RydeSmart technology." Inside the cab of every Ryder truck sits a little box that tracks the truck's location, speed, and fuel efficiency. It can even read and report back on "check engine" lights. It's a system that gives the driver quick and comprehensive information to make smart and timely decisions. It's like having a truck doctor on board who's continually diagnosing the patient and offering prescriptive help. And followers of Jesus who are, every day, leaning into an abiding, dependent relationship with him can trust the "Ryder Box" inside them, otherwise known as the Holy Spirit.

"While in university one of my professors, Dr. Fee, came one evening as a guest speaker for a weekly get-together in our residence hall. He surprised us when he shared his thoughts on prayer. He rocked our skeptical understanding of prayer by teaching us how to pray the Lord's Prayer not as a rote prayer to repeat, but as a guide for speaking honestly and conversationally with Jesus. He challenged us to put each phrase of the Lord's Prayer in our own words—to follow it like you would follow a recipe for baking a cake, sticking to the main ingredients but experimenting as well. That was 50 years ago, and I still pray that prayer almost every day of my life. I've learned these beautiful words are still the essential ingredients of authentic intimacy with Jesus. Not just intimacy from my limited and often selfish perspective of things, but intimacy grounded in who he is." —Floyd McClung

When we are branches abiding in the Vine, we pay better attention to what Jesus says and does, and how others react to him, simply to get to know him more deeply. And in knowing him we see him better, and in seeing him better we trust in him more deeply, and in trusting him more deeply we align ourselves with him, and in aligning ourselves with him we live our lives in an atmosphere of sensitivity to his Spirit. In the Jesus-centered life we trust the Holy Spirit, not our suspect ability to propel our own growth or manage our sin. Instead of following formulas or recipes, we follow the Spirit—this is what "divine anticipation" (one of the "four acts of love") means.

A few summers ago, Colorado youth pastor Josh Jones launched his youth group out of its summer-mission-trip rut. Every year he and his students would load up the church's 12-passenger van and head south for the 28-hour trek to Mexico and a weeklong work camp. And every year, as they traveled through countless towns on the way to their mission location, they saw dozens of opportunities to serve people that they were forced to pass by. Those on-the-way possibilities planted the seed of an idea in Josh. His group had already spent months studying all the ways that followers of Jesus depend upon the guidance of the Spirit of Jesus in their everyday lives. So Josh and his leaders planned something they called The Magical Mystery Tour—a mission trip that had no planned destination.

And that's the thing about getting to know Jesus: If you don't need him, you won't know him.

Here's how Josh describes what they did: "Because we'd been learning about dependence on the Holy Spirit, we decided we didn't need a 'destination' for our trip. Simply, we decided to ask the Holy Spirit to lead us to where he wanted us to go. We had no destination in mind and no plans for where we were going to stay or eat—all we had were a lot of 'what ifs' and a trailer-full of supplies hitched to our van." In the end, Josh's group spent a week on the road trying to listen better to the Spirit of Jesus and then respond by *doing something*. They helped dozens of people along the way who had real needs—needs the Spirit knew about. And the big side benefit is that they got to know Jesus much, much better, simply because they were depending on him so much. And that's the thing about getting to know Jesus: If you don't need him, you won't know him.

Jesus was always plunging his disciples into dependent experiences—situations that funneled them into a "desperate for you" relationship with him. The more they needed him, the more they came to know him. In Matthew 10, when Jesus sent out the Twelve two-by-two on their first ministry trip without him, he gave us a template for dependent living...

1. **Start with a doable challenge.** "These twelve Jesus sent out with the following instructions: 'Do not go among the Gentiles or

enter any town of the Samaritans. Go rather to the lost sheep of Israel' " (Matthew 10:5-6, NIV). Rather than forcing them into a cross-cultural challenge or an environment of stiff resistance, Jesus starts his disciples off in familiar surroundings with familiar people. Later on they'll go to the ends of the earth, but for now the challenge to risk and depend on the Spirit needs to be small enough to ensure some level of success.

When I was learning how to be a street evangelist in Europe, our trainers started us off by teaching us a discussion-starting drama we could perform to attract a crowd. The first place we did it was a public piazza in Rome that was well-known as a gathering place for young people interested in conversation with Americans. All of us were already scared to do something that seemed so risky, but we were not overwhelmed by our dependent challenge because we started with baby steps. We did the drama, and it provided an easy way to strike up a conversation with strangers. The bridge from shy, scared, awkward Americans to international missionaries was relatively easy because our leaders understood how to give us a taste of dependent living, not fire-hose us with it. The same progression holds true in our everyday lives—a doable challenge means we find an on-ramp into a conversation by asking people simple questions about their beliefs, or offering them a random act of kindness, or simply paying peculiar attention to their response when we ask how they're doing.

"I use my time alone in the car to just talk to Jesus—I talk about everything as honestly as I possibly can, until I feel I've been as raw as I can be." —Jo Saxton

2. **Look to Jesus to set specific boundaries for our risk.** "As you go, proclaim this message: 'The kingdom of heaven has come near.' Heal the sick, raise the dead, cleanse those who have leprosy, drive

out demons" (Matthew 10:7-8a, NIV). Jesus told his disciples exactly what to focus on when they spoke, and he gave them four ministry responsibilities that very definitely required them to depend on the power of God. He also, by the way, spent a lot of time modeling these responsibilities, giving them plenty of time to learn how to do them from the example of an incredible Mentor.

When we live in dependence, we can trust Jesus to set our boundaries.

In what areas is Jesus calling you to move on his behalf, and how is that specific calling defined by him? When I was just out of college, all of the "serious" followers of Jesus that I knew believed that he was going to call them into the hardest challenges they could imagine, because "hard" was the same as "God's will." But as I've grown older I've discovered that that simplistic belief is just not true. When we live in dependence, we can trust Jesus to set our boundaries—we don't rely on our preconceptions about what a true follower is supposed to do; we rely on the Spirit of Jesus to nudge us into the life he intends for us.

3. **Trust Jesus to meet our needs along the way.** "Freely you have received, freely give. Do not get any gold or silver or copper in your belts—no bag for the journey or extra shirt or sandals or a staff, for the worker is worth his keep" (Matthew 10:8b-10, NIV). Jesus understood that a dependent life is all about generosity—we give out of generous hearts, and we receive from God's generous heart. That means we give out of the fullness of what we've received and trust God to give us "manna" for our basic needs. Our generosity is a profound act of trust, and the more we trust Jesus, the more we camp out in his heart. The "Silent Generation" adults who grew up during the Great Depression have to wrestle through a default mindset that was formed by grinding deprivation—it's hard to be generous when you've had to scratch and scramble just to survive. That's an obvious and visceral example of a universal struggle: Those

who trust much, give much; those who are captives to fear hold onto what they have and guard it. It takes an extraordinary movement toward vulnerability to trust the provision of Jesus when you have every reason to guard your resources. That's why gifts of generosity are also acts of worship.

4. **Accept the trust Jesus has invested in us, and exercise your gifts.** "After Jesus had finished instructing his twelve disciples, he went on from there to teach and preach in the towns of Galilee" (Matthew 11:1, NIV). After Jesus had delivered his instructions to the disciples, he took off on his own ministry trip. Talk about communicating trust! Effectively, he was telling them he wasn't at all worried or anxious about how they'd fare on their adventure. He trusted them to experiment, risk, and learn as they went. And then he gathered them to debrief their experience and help them grow from it.

5. **Remember that dependence means that we look to Jesus as the source of our good impact.** When his disciples returned to download what happened on their ministry adventures, they told Jesus they were astonished by how God's Spirit had moved through them: "Lord, even the demons submit to us in your name" (Luke 10:17). And Jesus responded to their experience by offering a greater context for it: "I saw Satan fall like lightning from heaven. I have given you authority to trample on snakes and scorpions and to overcome all the power of the enemy; nothing will harm you. However, do not rejoice that the spirits submit to you, but rejoice that your names are written in heaven" (verses 18-20). Jesus is reminding his disciples that the power they experienced when they depended on the Spirit of God came directly from him (so don't get too impressed with yourselves). And he's refocusing their attention away from spiritual fireworks and onto what's really important—leading sheep that are caught in the brambles back to the safety of their true home.

When we grow in our dependence, moment to moment, on Jesus, then the greater things Jesus promised we'd do in our lives are entirely possible. And in our dependence on him, we come to know him through the portal of our hearts, not our heads.

18

Experiencing More, Automating Less

"It was not for our understanding, but our will, that Christ came. He who does that which he sees, shall understand; he who is set upon understanding rather than doing, shall go on stumbling and mistaking and speaking foolishness."

—George MacDonald

Researchers working for Volkswagen in Stockholm, Sweden, were searching to find ways to influence people to be more physically active in everyday life. We all know how fraught with broken promises and disaster most physical fitness efforts turn out to be. But these Swedes came up with something shrewd and inventive—and it really worked. At subway stops throughout the city, people can choose to ride the escalator up to the street level or climb the stairs. Predictably, most people choose the sedentary option of the escalator over the stairs. So, working all night, a swarming team of technicians transformed the stairs leading out of the Odenplan subway stop into a giant functioning piano keyboard. The steps, mapped to look exactly like the progression of black and white keys on a real piano, each produced the sound of a corresponding musical note when stepped on. Then the planners mounted video cameras at the base of the stairs so they could record what happened when commuters showed up in the morning.

After their initial surprise, travelers rushing to get to work stopped to consider the piano stairs, and then experimented with them. Many not only climbed the stairs, they also hopped around on them as they tried to play music instead of trudging their way up. Stair-climbing was transformed from a brainless inconvenience to a playful experience. Through the morning commute, Volkswagen researchers found that the musical stairs diverted 66 percent more people than normal onto the staircase and away from the escalator. And because of that, they managed to entice commuters into a fitness behavior they never would have considered otherwise. (To see this for yourself, search for it on YouTube using these words: "Piano Stairs Odenplan.") A playful and surprising experience re-engaged these commuters with the joy and satisfaction of physical exertion. They were not *disciplining* themselves to choose a healthier option; they were caught up in an experience that made them forget about the work of physical fitness.[1]

"Jesus has given me a kind of *charism*—to seek him, primarily in the mornings, by wandering around in a big, empty space and 'keeping him company.' We converse and express our love, and I get correction, instruction, and glimpses of him. He teases me, and reminds me of how fond he is of me. He expresses his ridiculous generosity toward me." —Bob Krulish

I've said we live in a culture of distraction that infiltrates all of the natural gaps in our lives, but we also live in a culture of automation that entices us to outsource our effort. The escalator at the Odenplan subway station was more popular than the stairs because it offloaded physical effort from commuters, keeping their muscles from the exercise they need to be strengthened. That effort is physically good for them, and we want what's good for people, so the conventional response is to *should* those commuters into better habits. But the Volkswagen researchers recognized the weak leveraging power of *should*, landing on an experiential solution instead. If our relationship with Jesus is going to move from a *should* that requires us to work at it, to an *adventure* that invites us to play, we'll need to experience him more and automate him less.

An automated relationship with Jesus replaces *doing things* with *talking about things.*

An automated relationship with Jesus replaces *doing things* with *talking about things*. We use our words about Jesus as an effort-reducing substitute for actually living like Jesus. I've been a word person my whole life, relying on my practiced ability to explore and describe things as a subtle replacement for *doing* the things I'm describing. Before I married Bev, one of the things she loved the most about me was my ability to talk deeply with her. But after our wedding, she soon understood how hollow words can be when they're not interwoven with vigorous doing. I didn't know it, but I'd learned to treat words as if they were actually the actions they represented. If I had a conversation about vulnerability with Bev, using eloquent words to describe its importance, but I wasn't actually vulnerable with her, she was left with an empty feeling—it's a kind of bait-and-switch. It got so bad that she was, at one point, disappointed by the long, wordy birthday cards I used to give her. Her heart longed for a richer *experience* with me, not a richer discourse.

It's safer to explore ideas about Jesus, or consider how tasty his recipes for Christian living are, than to actually know him and live like him experientially.

It's just as easy for us to live a bait-and-switch relationship with Jesus as it is with our other "lovers." It's safer to explore ideas about Jesus, or consider how tasty his recipes for Christian living are, than to actually know him and live like him experientially. Our conventional templates for relational growth—almost always some version of an information download—are fatally flawed, in much the same way my strategy for replacing actions with words was fatally flawed in my marriage. It's the difference between a description of what's in the center of a peanut butter cup and actually biting into one. Jesus modeled experiential living. Rather than...

- describing what it's like to walk on water, he invites Peter to do it with him;
- helping the "rich young ruler" to understand the benefits of following him, Jesus simply asks him to sell everything he owns and start walking with him;

• telling his disciples all the reasons they should offer mercy to others, he forgives the soldiers who are crucifying him;

• urging his followers to love their enemies and pray for those who persecute them, he accepts dinner invitations from his worst critics.

Innovative educators have long pointed to the power of experience as a catalyst for true growth. In a report on why so many American students are failing science, public radio education reporter Jenny Brundin says:

So what's going on in classrooms? Lots of talk about facts and procedures. And students mostly just listen. They don't get their hands on things, or they're often not required to figure things out on their own…[The key is] getting kids to think critically and invent, using real-world examples. Dissecting a frog or mixing chemicals in a beaker isn't enough. Research shows those lab exercises are more like following a recipe than discovering scientific principles… Students who discover the answers will remember them much better than if a teacher told them in a lecture.[2]

"Cultivate a relationship with Jesus through the pursuit of beauty that is experiential—through good writing, art (in its many forms), music, and being out in creation. These things are sensual, and incorporate a relationship with God that opens up the senses to the ways Jesus reveals himself through sound, smell, touch, taste, and sight. I enjoy photography that brings me to how light works, its majesty, and God's canvas. It reminds me of story because every picture is telling a story. I love watercolor painting for the same reasons—it defies expertise and keeps me the learner. I love fly-fishing because water is just beautiful, and I get to put what I catch back. It also feels so much more of an art than a science." —Steve Merritt

Simply, the more we experience or discover Jesus, and the more we imitate him in our lives, the more we grow. Skiing legend Jean-Claude Killy says: "The best and fastest way to learn a sport is to watch and imitate a champion."[3] Imitation can seem like a false path to true growth, but it's actually a potent way to move from automating something to experiencing something. When we experience Jesus, and then imitate the way he teaches and relates to others instead of automating him with our words, we soon discover that we're growing more like him. For example, this automating-to-experiencing shift might look like this...

FROM...	TO...
Praying for others by asking them what they need, and then brainstorming our prayer based on what *we know*.	Praying for others by asking Jesus first how to pray for them, then waiting for his direction before we open our mouth. This is prayer that's based on what *he* knows, and supercharges our prayer time by making it surprising, fun, and experiential.
Complaining and gossiping about the people who frustrate or thwart or make us angry— the people who behave like enemies in our lives.	Asking Jesus for creative, surprising help to respond to these "enemies" by loving them (with no preconceptions about what love might mean), or at least praying for them (again, seeking his direction in how to pray, first).
Assuming Jesus has no interest in the inconsequential, "unspiritual" aspects of our daily lives.	Inviting him into everything, no matter how small or insignificant. That includes talking to Jesus about how to carry ourselves when we're late for an appointment, or soliciting his creativity when we're deciding what to make for a meal, or even asking for help when we need a parking spot (often wrongly described as a shallow expression of prayer). If it matters to us, then it's all worth talking about with Jesus. And his participation in the inconsequential makes it all consequential.
Summoning our own courage and determination when we face daunting challenges or difficult people.	Finding an "alone space" to literally raise our arms to Jesus, like a child would, and asking him to empower our words and actions so that we leave a taste of him behind.

FROM...	TO...
Making small talk at a public gathering or neighborhood party or business function.	Asking Jesus to show us how to engage each person we meet, including the type of topic to bring up or the questions to ask. In the midst of our conversations we breathe a silent prayer: "Jesus, who would you like me to pursue, and how would you like me to do it?" We do this so often that we forget we're praying.
Strategizing about needs or decisions or opportunities by weighing the pros and cons, and then making a gut decision.	Waiting in silence first for the Spirit's guidance and insight—expecting to receive a word or a picture or a phrase or a sense of peace about the direction we need to go.
Debating with yourself, back and forth, about what's right to do in any given situation.	Simply doing the *one thing* you already know is right to do, because the Spirit of Jesus is in you, nudging. We often automate our relationship with Jesus—remove effort from it—by circling decisions until we neutralize them. An experiential relationship, instead, means we act on what we already know to do, because he's already made some things clear to us.

Perhaps the biggest way that we automate our relationship with Jesus is our common practice of one-sided prayer. A.W. Tozer asks: "If you do all the talking when you pray, how will you ever hear God's answers?"[4] If our goal is to discover and experience Jesus, we'll have to listen to him at least as much as we talk to him. We ask more questions, and make fewer pronouncements. We experience truth, not merely describe it from behind the glass.

Endnotes

1 Claire Bates, "Scaling New Heights: Piano Stairway Encourages Commuters to Ditch the Escalators," *Daily Mail*, October 11, 2009.

2 Jenny Brundin, "Science in Colorado Classrooms: Big Bang or Black Hole?—Part 1," Colorado Public Radio, October 5, 2012.

3 Paul G. Schempp, "Teaching Sport and Physical Activity: Insights on the Road to Excellence" *Human Kinetics*, 2003, 122.

4 A.W. Tozer, *Voice of a Prophet: Who Speaks for God?* (Bethany House Publishers, 2014), 30.

19

Scaring Yourself for Good

"Hold me Jesus, 'cause I'm shaking like a leaf."

—Rich Mullins

As I've mentioned, after college I joined an international missionary training school to learn how to connect with people and talk to them about Jesus. I lived in Rome for three months during the school, and then our team traveled south for three weeks of outreach experience. One night in Sicily, during an evangelistic event, a woman came screaming and flailing into our midst, apparently possessed by a demon. I'm not kidding—it was like something out of a movie. There was no time to consult with demon-dealing experts at that point. My friends and I had to trust that the Spirit of Jesus would show us what to do right then. So we prayed and asked for help. Then we prayed over this scary woman as best we could (in English, a language she didn't understand), trusting Jesus to assert his authority over any oppressive spirits. And the woman promptly stopped screaming and frothing and thrashing. She became calm, as if someone had flipped a switch inside her. We stood amazed at the power of God, and we were drawn more deeply into relationship with Jesus because we'd partnered to pull this whole thing off.

In practical terms, a dependent relationship with Jesus means scaring ourselves, in a good way.

It was a scary experience, but all of us felt alive because of it—and close to Jesus. In practical terms, a dependent relationship with Jesus means scaring ourselves, in a good way. It means taking risks to serve others when the Spirit of Jesus nudges us. It might mean volunteering to lead something that you'd normally not lead, or serving in a setting that's far outside your comfort zone, or reaching out to people whose problems are beyond your ability to solve, or talking to your friends about the real Jesus. Scaring ourselves by taking risks in our relationship with Jesus runs counter to our natural fear of danger, and it runs counter to our culture's constant drumbeat regarding safety.

"I see Jesus in others, so I can serve them as if I were serving him (Mathew 25:35-40)." —Jonathan Salgado

In Western society, we talk a lot about safety, probably more than you realize. Because our psychological reality is much broader than our physical reality—I mean, both our conventional media and our social media expose us to an overwhelming number of "threats" from outside our current physical reality—we have been trained to fear for our safety as a matter of everyday life. Because we are exposed to fearful, threatening things all over the world, and our brains aren't good at compartmentalizing real fears away from outlandish or unrealistic fears, we're always on "fear overload." I live just 20 minutes away from the sites of two of the most horrific acts of violence in U.S. history: the Columbine High School massacre and the Aurora movie theater shooting. Both were mass killings by psychopathic terrorists, victimizing helpless people. A few days after the theater shootings, President Barack Obama was speaking to the National Urban League in New Orleans. He'd already flown to Denver earlier in the week to meet with victims, police officers, and medical personnel. He was angry, so he closed with this charge: *We should…recognize that we have no greater mission as a country than keeping our young people safe.*[1]

Now, that's a normal thing to say after the trauma of a mass murder. But it's also not true (and I have no political "skin" in the game here). Keeping ourselves or others safe is *not* our greatest mission in life. This lofty-sounding truism undermines the clear mandate of a gospel message that urges us to set captives free, whatever the cost. In *A Failure of Nerve*, author Edwin Friedman urges leaders to prefer boldness and adventure over safety. Friedman points to a cultural legacy that is marked by brave adventurers who changed the course of history because they eschewed a safety mentality, choosing instead to promote…

- maturity over more data;
- stamina over new techniques; and
- personal responsibility over empathy.[2]

A rich life is always driven by something that's worth dying for—this is the essential mission of our calling as ruined-for-Jesus people.

We cannot move into the world fueled by the redemptive mission of Jesus when we repeatedly lift up safety as more important than any other thing in life. Jesus is blunt about this: "For whoever wishes to save his life will lose it; but whoever loses his life for My sake will find it" (Matthew 16:25). A rich life is always driven by something that's worth dying for—this is the essential mission of our calling as ruined-for-Jesus people. It's no accident that all of Jesus' disciples lived to die. Paul spells it out in his manifesto to the church in Rome: "For I consider that the sufferings of this present time are not worthy to be compared with the glory that is to be revealed to us" (Romans 8:18). When we respond to the promptings of the Spirit by taking risks that scare us, we are losing our life to find it. Practically, we follow Friedman's advice to live more adventurously, scaring ourselves for good, when we…

- **Value maturity more than gathering additional data.** Maturity is really a pragmatic response to what's needed in any given situation. In the case of my experience with the demon-possessed woman in Sicily, our little team could've searched around for somebody who had more experience with this sort of thing, or we could've debated whether the woman was truly possessed or was having a psychological episode. Instead, maturity in this situation demanded that we attempt to meet the practical need in front of us—we asked Jesus to help us, and then we took authority over the demonic presence that was assaulting her. Maturity means we step into situations to meet needs, depending on the Spirit of Jesus to give us the resources to do it. Gathering additional data is often our cloaked way of diverting attention away from simply acting on the hard things we know must be done.

• **Exercise stamina more than pursue new techniques.** It sounds funny, but sometimes we look for new tips and techniques to solve problems for us and for others instead of sticking it out in a difficult situation. I used to take my daughter to the corner bus stop every morning, where all the other parents stood around making small talk for 10 minutes or so while we waited. I'm terrible at small talk, so I always felt awkward and like an outsider at the stop. Day after day I'd come back from the corner disappointed in myself for my deficits in the small talk tips-and-techniques department. But one day I realized my primary need was not to grow in a conversation technique that doesn't really match my personality, but to ask Jesus to give me the courage to initiate and persevere in conversations with people at the stop. Jesus was calling me to simply ask one question of one person every day at that bus stop, and then stick with the conversation to see what would happen. "Scaring myself for good" meant, simply, exercising stamina in my relationships with people who, frankly, scared me because they could do something that I did poorly.

• **Practice personal responsibility more than empathy.** Empathy sounds like a universally good thing—who doesn't want to be the sort of person who not only feels concern for others but actually enters into their emotional reality? But when we do that, we create a safe place for others to stay stuck in the emotional reality that is impeding their growth and holding them captive. Empathy leads us to ask: *How can I occupy this person's emotional space?* Personal responsibility, on the other hand, leads us to ask: *What do I have to give here?* That's counterintuitive, because we've been taught that empathy is our greatest gift to others.

Ⓙ

"Failure, disappointment, sorrow, and loss have been great teachers. They have dragged me to Jesus—most often unwillingly. Perhaps these friends have served me more faithfully than any others in my desire for Jesus and my need for Jesus." —Bob Krulish

Here's a simple illustration of this. When we got Pippin, a new teddy bear hamster for my youngest daughter, my big-hearted wife saw that Chloe, our little bichon frisé dog, was very, very eager to inspect the new member of the family. Because Bev felt empathy for Chloe's whimpering pleas to get up close and personal with Pippin, she wanted to let our dog get a good sniff of the hamster. I protested, insisting that this was one situation where we had to exercise "personal responsibility" and ignore our empathy for Chloe. On the sly, my wife did the deed anyway—convinced by her empathy to fulfill our dog's need to "meet" Pippin—and was shocked when Chloe suddenly tried to chomp off the hamster's head. Empathy, in this case, almost cost a hamster her life. Personal responsibility means that we do something that scares us almost more than anything else—disappoint people (and maybe even dogs) on purpose, because we care more about helping them grow, and what's ultimately good for them, than sharing their emotional space.

We are all called to go into the cave on behalf of others—to enter into situations and relationships that scare us, so that we can give what we have to give.

Scaring ourselves for good is a heroic way to live. In the movie version of J.R.R. Tolkien's book *The Return of the King*, the hero Aragorn intends to enter the mountain tomb of disgraced warriors—ghosts who cannot find rest because they behaved as cowards in their last battle—to recruit these wraiths in a last great battle against evil. Aragorn's friends Legolas and Gimli spy him sneaking away on this quest, and they join him. When they arrive at the gates of the dead, their horses are so panicked that they bolt and run.

The mouth of the cave smells like death. And Aragorn, turning to his friends, says, "I am not afraid of death" and plunges into the darkness.[3] We are all called to go into the cave on behalf of others—to enter into situations and relationships that scare us, so that we can give what we have to give. But we won't do this if we value safety and certainty over boldness and adventure.

Endnotes

1 From remarks made by President Barack Obama to the National Urban League Conference, on July 25, 2012.

2 Friedman, *A Failure of Nerve*, 33.

3 From the shooting script of *The Lord of the Rings: The Two Towers* (2002), written by Fran Walsh and adapted from J.R.R. Tolkien's *The Two Towers* (New York: Ballantine Books, 1965). The film was directed by Peter Jackson.

20

Asking 'Where Would Jesus Be?'

"Obedience is the road to all things—the only way in which to grow able to trust him. Love and faith and obedience are sides of the same prism."

—George MacDonald

My friend Ron Belsterling, a longtime professor of youth and family studies at Nyack College in New York, also serves as a youth pastor at his local church. One year, he decided to replace his youth group's traditional overseas mission trip with a local inner-city outreach. Near the end of their outreach, the small team of students looked out their mission organization's window at night and saw two men viciously kicking a woman who was high on drugs, and therefore unable to defend herself or run away.

Ron turned to his suburban, middle-class teenagers and asked, "What are we going to do about this?" His students said, "Well, we can't go down there!" And Ron answered, "Why not? *Down there* is where Jesus would be." The students responded: "What can we do? The only thing we know how to do is sing!" (Most of the students on the outreach were part of the church's youth choir.) Ron fired back, "Well, let's go down there and sing, then. We'll give what Jesus has given us to give." So the whole group trooped down to the street and started singing. The two guys kicking the woman looked up, startled, and ran away in fear. The woman crawled across the street and lay down in the middle of the kids as they sang.

That night, those students followed the beeline to Jesus that Ron found for them. They learned what it's like to follow the nudge of the Spirit and offer rescue to a woman in trouble, just as Jesus did with the woman caught in adultery in John 8. Ron didn't ask, "What would Jesus do?" He asked, instead, "*Where* would Jesus be?"

But if we carry the Spirit of Jesus in us, and his presence is what transforms people, then our *where* is much more important than our *what* and *how*.

Because *doing* is elevated over *being* in Western culture, it's natural that we're more interested in *performance* than *presence*. But if we carry the Spirit of Jesus in us, and his presence is what transforms people, then our *where* is much more important than our *what* and *how*. Put another way, this means that following God's will is less about figuring out the specifics of what Jesus wants us to do in life—what matters more is *where* he wants us to be, because we'll carry him with us wherever we go. When Ron saw a helpless woman getting beat up in a bad part of town, he didn't know what he and his ill-qualified teenagers were going to do, but he knew where they needed to be. Once we find our *where*, the Spirit will work out our *what* and *how*.

In Leo Tolstoy's short story "The Three Questions," a king is on a quest for wisdom. He wants to know:

1. When is the best time to do each thing?

2. Who are the most important people to work with?

3. What is the most important thing to do at all times?

As the king asks his questions, the answers his advisers give him are wildly divergent. So the king decides to visit a wise hermit he's heard about—the man lives in a nearby village. Because it's well-known that the hermit only meets with commoners, the king must leave his personal guard behind and disguise himself as a peasant. When the king arrives, the hermit is digging in his flowerbeds. The king asks the man to answer his three questions, but he gets only silence in response. So, not knowing what else to do, he begins digging, too. He works alongside the hermit for a long time and finally decides to ask his questions again. But before the hermit can answer, a man with a severe wound plunges out of the underbrush and collapses near them. The king shifts his attention to the injured man, caring for him the rest of that day and evening. By the next day, the man has improved. He recognizes the king through his disguise and confesses that he'd been on a mission to kill the king because of a past grievance. Before he could get close enough to carry out his plan, one of the king's guards wounded him. Because the king has cared for him and saved his life, the man disavows his murderous plan and pledges his allegiance.

"I pay attention to stories of Jesus working in the lives of people in more dramatic ways around the world." —Craig Blomberg

Finally, the king returns to the hermit to ask his three questions. And the hermit breaks his silence and replies that the king has already received his answers:

1. The most important time is now.

2. The most important person is whoever you are with.

3. The most important thing is to do good to the person you are with.[1]

These are "Where would Jesus be?" answers. Tolstoy's parable underscores this beeline-to-Jesus truth: When we live under the influence of the Spirit of Jesus, our *where* is more important than our *how*. We know this is at the core of Jesus' heart, because the Incarnation—God taking on the form of man and "moving into the neighborhood"—is the greatest act of heroism any of us will ever know, and it was driven by *where*.

In January 2012, the massive cruise ship Costa Concordia ran into a submerged rock off the western coast of Italy, ripping a large gash in its side and filling the engine room with water. The flooding cut power to the ship, and the 1,000-foot, skyscraper-tall behemoth drifted and ran aground near Giglio Island. There were more than 4,200 people on board, and it took an agonizing six hours to evacuate the ship, even though it sat half-sunk in shallow water just 500 yards from land. Because of the chaotic and prolonged rescue operation, 32 people lost their lives on that ship. After a $1.5 billion salvage operation successfully refloated the boat and towed it to a salvage yard in Genoa, all but one of the dead had been recovered. That missing man's name was Russel Rebello, a 33-year-old waiter from India. For almost three years after the wreck of the Costa Concordia, Russel's brother Kevin traveled back and forth from his home in Milan to the coast, where he talked to salvage operators and local residents about the search for his brother's body.

"I hang out with the poor, marginalized, and friends-in-pain—to hear their stories. Every time—*every time*—I feel Jesus in the midst."
—Kathy Escobar

Kevin told the people he met: "I've not lost hope. I know the official search stopped a long time ago but I will continue to look for my brother's body. I watch every news bulletin or program on the Concordia in the hope of finding some piece of information that will help me find my brother."[2] If you are not the brother of Russel Rebello, then your assessment of the Costa Concordia debacle is simple—4,200 people were accounted for, and the body of an Indian waiter you'd never heard of remains missing and probably lost forever. *But if you are the brother of Russel Rebello, then you are living in the momentum and the reality of the Good Shepherd, who is Jesus.* "If a man has a hundred sheep and one of them wanders away," Jesus asks his followers, "what will he do? Won't he leave the ninety-nine others on the hills and go out to search for the one that is lost? And if he finds it, I tell you the truth, he will rejoice over it more than over the ninety-nine that didn't wander away! In the same way, it is not my heavenly Father's will that even one of these little ones should perish" (Matthew 18:12-14, NLT).

Kevin Rebello remained focused on the one who was lost because his heart was intimately tied to his brother, and he wouldn't rest until Russel's body was finally found (in November 2014, by salvage operators working on the eighth deck of the Costa Concordia). And likewise, Jesus is determined to find his own lost brothers and sisters who have gone missing—his focus is, first, on the whereabouts of the lost ones. His *where* is not with the 99 who are grazing peacefully on the hillside; it's with the one who got distracted and left behind, or decided on its own to find better places to graze, or reacted to a threat by running away from the Shepherd rather than to him.

Jesus is determined to find his own lost brothers and sisters who have gone missing—his focus is, first, on the whereabouts of the lost ones.

The brother of Russel Rebello did not rest until he found his beloved, even though there was no hope he'd be found alive. "No hope" is not a deal-breaker if the depth of your love and your commitment to the beloved goes deep. Maybe you feel like a dead person inside—the forgettable and forgotten Indian waiter on a ship that never should have sunk in the first place. Maybe you feel like no one cares enough to pursue the dead man on the ship. Well, Jesus (who exactly mirrors the heart of a God we can't see) will not rest until he tracks down and offers rescue to every single sheep who has strayed from the flock. And all of us, at one time or another, fit that definition. We are all Russel Rebello, and Jesus is our relentless brother. None of us remains safely, throughout our lifetime, with the 99 on the hills. We have all been cut off from the protection of the flock by sin. And it doesn't matter if we feel hopeless or others tell us we are lost forever, because Jesus generates his own hope. And so, as we are propelled by the heart of Jesus, we will...

• Never assume we, or others, are just a face in the crowd—we will live our lives with a focus on the individual, always.

• Give the treasure of our determined hope to people who've been given-up on by others.

• Leave the *where* of the safely grazing masses to pursue the *where* of the wandered-away individual, when it is inconvenient and costly and even dangerous.

• Act like owners, not mere caretakers, of the sheep Jesus has given us in our pastures (that means the friends, enemies, and family members who populate our lives). We do not punch a time clock when it comes to others' needs. Sometimes we are wakened in the night by the unacceptable lostness of a sheep, and we redouble our pursuit as the Spirit of Jesus leads us.

• Determine to pursue others in the spirit of the wartime cry of Winston Churchill: "Never give up. Never, never, never give up." The only trump card to "Never give up" is when the Spirit shows us that our pursuit is no longer what the pursued most needs.

• See the unique value of every single sheep and refuse to let one stray, because the whole would suffer in its absence.

• Lay down our lives for those who can never repay such a gift, and may not ever acknowledge the cost of it.

When we ask ourselves, in the midst of everyday life, "Where would Jesus be?" and then act on what we know, we get the *what* and the *how* thrown in. If our lives are determined by the *where* of the wandering and needy sheep, we will leave safer pastures for the wild unknown. The Apostle Paul describes what this kind of life is like:

We patiently endure troubles and hardships and calamities of every kind. We have been beaten, been put in prison, faced angry mobs, worked to exhaustion, endured sleepless nights, and gone without food. We prove ourselves by our purity, our understanding, our patience, our kindness, by the Holy Spirit within us, and by our sincere love. We faithfully preach the truth. God's power is working in us. We use the weapons of righteousness in the right hand for attack and the left hand for defense. We serve God whether people honor us or despise us, whether they slander us or praise us. We are honest, but they call us impostors. We are ignored, even though we are well known. We live close to death, but we are still alive. We have been beaten, but we have not been killed. Our hearts ache, but we always have joy. We are poor, but we give spiritual riches to others. We own nothing, and yet we have everything (2 Corinthians 6:4b-10, NLT).

The context, for Paul, is clear—he wants the lost and wandering Corinthians to come when he calls: "I am asking you to respond as if you were my own children. Open your hearts to us!" (verse 13). Love compels him to carry his hope to wherever the sheep have wandered, and that determined pursuit gives him tunnel vision—he patiently endures the angry mobs and prison sentences and hunger pangs and sleepless nights because the hope he carries in him overshadows all of it. And that hope, personified in Jesus, drives him to be where the needy need him most—that means *wherever* the Spirit leads him.

Endnotes

1 Leo Tolstoy, "The Three Questions," from the collection of short stories *What Men Live By and Other Tales*, translated by L. and A. Maude (a Project Gutenburg ebook, June 13, 2009).

2 Quoted in the Sky News report by Nick Pisa, "Costa Concordia: Hunt for Russel Rebello's Body," on January 12, 2013.

21

Waking Up to Metaphor

"Poets do not go mad; but chess-players do. Mathematicians go mad, and cashiers; but creative artists very seldom. I am not, as will be seen, in any sense attacking logic: I only say that this danger does lie in logic, not in imagination."

—G.K. Chesterton

Uprooted plants. Blind guides who fall into ditches. Lost sheep. Throwing good food to dogs... Jesus described these things in the Bible, *but they never actually happened.* That's because they're all metaphors. And Jesus LOVED using metaphors when he taught—the four I just listed show up in *one* random chapter in one gospel account (Matthew 15). A metaphor is symbolic language—it's a description of something we understand well, used to give context and meaning to something we don't understand well.

Jesus gravitated to metaphors because he was determined to translate the character of God, and what life is like in the kingdom of God, to "foreigners." In the Hebrews 11 listing of Old Testament heroes who were martyred for their faith, the people of God are described as "foreigners and nomads here on earth" (Hebrews 11:13). That's not just hyperbole—we are born into a world marred by sin, yet we are meant to live as sons and daughters in "our Father's house." We don't know much about our native land because we've been formed by the assumptions and sensibilities and values of our twisted context.

And so, what would a good and generous God do to help his beloved children know the truth about his heart and the truth about his kingdom? Well, he'd use the power of metaphor, and he'd embed those metaphors all around us in the hope that we would draw near to him even when we are oblivious to him. In Romans 1, Paul rolls out this little grenade:

> [Wicked people] know the truth about God because he has made it obvious to them. For ever since the world was created, people have seen the earth and sky. Through everything God made, they can clearly see his invisible qualities—his eternal power and divine nature. So they have no excuse for not knowing God (Romans 1:19-20, NLT).

Slow down and pay attention here... Paul is saying that all of the created world is embedded with clues to the heart of God—his power and nature. And those "invisible qualities" form the foundation for the kingdom of God. Creation itself is teeming with metaphors that point to the character of God and what life is like in his kingdom. We will find them if we choose to pay attention.

Paul is saying that all of the created world is embedded with clues to the heart of God—his power and nature.

The Jesus-centered life is, at its core, a life that's lived awake. I mean, the dull ache and responsibility of everyday life is trying to turn us into sleepwalkers. Every day we walk through the gates of Disneyland but hardly ever notice the attractions because we have acclimated ourselves to wonderland over time, and it has slowly receded into the background. We are bent on achieving and surviving and controlling and entertaining ourselves, and we have forgotten that the story of God is not only embedded in the life of Jesus, but in the life of his creation.

"I treat all of life as an opportunity to worship." —Derwin Gray

Ever wonder why the time you spend in nature—hiking or fishing or running or walking or camping or hunting or skiing or birdwatching or biking—has such an immersive impact on your soul? Well, when we surround ourselves with earth and sky, we start to see a little more clearly. My friend and pastor Tom Melton created a word to describe a life that is awake to beauty and metaphor—he calls himself an "apprecianado." That means he is an aficionado of appreciation. And I think he's landed on the antidote to the zombie life we've been lulled into. Annie Dillard says:

...there seems to be such a thing as beauty, a grace wholly gratuitous...If these tremendous events are random combinations of matter run amok, the yield of millions of monkeys at millions of typewriters, then what is it in us, hammered out of those same typewriters, that they ignite? We must somehow take a wider view, look at the whole landscape, really see it, and describe what's going on here. Then we can at least wail the right question into the swaddling band of darkness, or, if it comes to that, choir the proper praise.[1]

When we slow down to truly appreciate the created world that surrounds us, the metaphors God has embedded about himself emerge from the background. Nature has God's fingerprints all over it, but it is not God himself. So, if all of creation is shot-through with metaphors for the character and sensibilities of Jesus, here's how you can find and nurture your inner apprecianado...

When we slow down to truly appreciate the created world that surrounds us, the metaphors God has embedded about himself emerge from the background.

• **Treat everything as if it's a metaphor, because it is.** If everything God made has at least one metaphor for his power and divine nature locked up in it, simply slow down to pay attention to it. That leaf, that tree, that rock, those squirrels, that spider, that flower, those weather patterns, that stream, that hawk, those ants…they are all screaming something true about God. One way to think about this is to remember the way Jesus is a perfect mirror image of the God we can't see—the created world is also a perfect mirror image of the God we can't see. It may sound goofy, but it's simply accepting what Paul is saying, and living out that truth as if it *was* true. To do this, you'll have to bring what is in the background into the foreground. You will have to give yourself permission to enjoy this luxury—stop every now and then to study the created things that surround you. Stop. Get close enough to notice something. Pay attention as if the thing you're looking at is a teacher. And then…

• **Ask one fundamental question, over and over.** As you are moving through God's creation with the heart of an apprecianado, you are asking the Spirit of Jesus the same question, over and over: *Show me your power and divine nature.* You stare with particular attention at one aspect of what God has made, not at an entire landscape. Or you listen or taste or smell with the same peculiar attention. And then you ask Jesus to reveal some truth about himself in the thing you're fixed upon. Then wait in silence. Don't brainstorm an insight; let Jesus simply give one to you. And it will come if you are expecting it. When you get used to asking this question in the slowed-down pauses of your life, the world (and Jesus) will come alive to you in a way it hasn't before. Your radar will be up, all the time, and your pursuit of the character and sensibilities of Jesus will open up new remembered truths about him.

We treat so much of the beauty in our lives as merely the backdrop to our personal drama—painted scenery that frames the aria in our opera.

• **Cultivate a passion for beauty.** An apprecianado will stop in the presence of beauty to drink it in. We treat so much of the beauty in our lives as merely the backdrop to our personal drama—painted scenery that frames the aria in our opera. On my nightly walks around our circle-drive neighborhood with my wife and ridiculous bichon frisé, I often stop—mid-sentence—to notice something beautiful: "Do you notice that...moon or looming tree or bright star or smell of a fireplace or rustle of a rabbit in the bushes?" Then I describe what I'm noticing and how it's impacting me. And then I'm asking Jesus to show me his power and divine nature. It's amazing how natural this rhythm becomes, once you've done it a few times.

"I need time alone in the outdoors—there's something healing and refreshing and reconnecting about being outside for me. I love to go fishing, but mostly I'm just hanging out by the side of the river looking at the water rushing by, watching an eagle swoop down overhead, listening to the chipmunks chatter and reconnecting with the awe of our creator—the one who holds it all together by his very Word."
—Carl Medearis

• **Taste and see.** The psalmist tells us to "taste and see that the Lord is good" (Psalm 34:8). You'll move your life from a dull sleepwalk to an adventure if you take these sorts of pronouncements more literally. I've led hundreds of people through a simple tasting experience that seems undoubtedly weird at first, but not so weird once they give in and do it. I offer them an array of disparate tastes in little cups and ask them to sample three of them. Then I ask them to choose the taste that interests them the most and sample it further. As they do, I ask them to ask Jesus this question: "What does this taste say about you—some aspect of your goodness?" Then they wait in silence for the Spirit of Jesus to reveal truth. And then I give them a little slip of paper to fill out. Here it is:

Jesus, the taste of _____ reminds me that you are
_____, and you show me your goodness when you
_____.

Then I play some music in the background and ask them to proclaim in a very loud voice whatever they've written on their slips. I have them do it one after the other, rapidly. And the room is full of praise, a crescendo of beauty that is unlike any worship experience I've ever been involved with.

Pay attention to the rich tastes of your life, and ask Jesus to show you the metaphors of taste that describe him in what you are eating or drinking. It won't be weird for long, once you give yourself permission to do it.

• **Respond with worship.** The exclamation point at the end of every appreciando experience is worship. Once a metaphor becomes clear to you, pointing to the beauty and truth of Jesus, simply praise him for it. As we thank him for revealing himself all around us, we wake ourselves up just a little more. And the awake life is the Jesus-centered life.

Endnotes

1 Annie Dillard, *Pilgrim at Tinker Creek* (New York, NY: Harper Perennial Modern Classics, 2013), 9-10.

22

Fearlessly Engaging

"It is impossible to stress too strongly that the beginning of mission is not an action of ours, but the presence of a new reality, the presence of the Spirit of God in power."

—Lesslie Newbigin

In the Jesus-centered life, our deepening attachment to Jesus creates a pathway for his life to flow into our dead branch, producing fruit that can nourish others. Slowly, surely, and in our own messy ways, we begin to say and do things prompted by the Spirit of Jesus living within us. And that means that the way we engage others moves from cautious to fearless, for the sake of their freedom.

I was never in a garage band, but whenever I hear a phrase that sounds like the name of a garage band (my daughter said the phrase "dissected squid juice" the other day, for example), I tell people that it was actually the name of my band when I was in high school. I'm guessing I've now told people that I've been a member of more than a thousand garage bands when I was a teenager. That might be psychotic behavior, but I wish I was the kind of guy who'd been in a garage band called Dissected Squid Juice. Playing improvised music with friends has a magnetic attraction to my soul. Even though I've never been in a band, I've played with thousands of people in my own version of an improvisational and creative collaboration, leading them through my "Jesus-Centered Ministry" training. This eight-hour experience is characterized by a constant flow of interaction—in pairs, trios, tables, and the whole group. I give context and direction and lots of feedback to these conversations, but the output is always a surprise, and therefore my responses are always improvised in the moment. The best garage-band players find ways to integrate their distinct voice into the band's collective voice, and the best conversations have Jesus as their focus and an improvisational, risk-taking interplay among the players.

The corollary to Jesus' "You don't have because you don't ask" is this: "You don't understand because you don't pay attention."

In our home, my wife and I lead a small group of senior highers (including our daughter Lucy) in a Sunday afternoon pursuit of Jesus. After one gathering, my wife (rather tentatively) asked me, "Do you *like* leading this group?" And I answered, "Are you kidding me? I *love* it… It's my favorite thing to do…" Nothing's more energizing and satisfying than a long garage-band-jam of a conversation. These kinds of conversations are the fields in which all good things grow. And fearless conversations offer the best soil, and therefore grow the best crops. When we engage others fearlessly, we're making beautiful music together. What infuses ordinary conversations with a fearless sort of yeast? Well, for starters:

• **We pay "ridiculous attention" to others.** In addition to paying ridiculous attention to Jesus, we do the same when we're engaging others. The corollary to Jesus' "You don't have because you don't ask" is this: "You don't understand because you don't pay attention." Paying attention—or paying attention so well that we could call it "ridiculous"—is one of the greatest acts of humble service we can offer one another. Most people, most days, don't have anyone paying ridiculous attention to what they say or do.

• **We ask more demanding questions.** I don't mean we ask questions in a demanding way; I mean we ask questions that make others wrestle with the truth, explore what they believe, and see Jesus differently than they have before. I've mentioned that Jesus asked questions all the time—he was constantly responding to questions with questions of his own. If you count every question he asked in the four Gospels (Matthew, Mark, Luke, and John) you come up with an astonishing number: 287! And these weren't easy-answer questions. For example:

- "Which is easier: to say to this paralyzed man, 'Your sins are forgiven,' or to say, 'Get up, take your mat and walk?' " (Mark 2:9, NIV).
- "Salt is good, but if it loses its saltiness, how can you make it salty again?" (Mark 9:50a, NIV).
- "Why do you call me good?" (Mark 10:18a, NIV).

If we pay close attention to the kinds of questions Jesus asked, we notice they were always *surprising, specific,* and *personal.* And the more surprising, specific, and personal the questions we ask others, the more likely we are to start or propel a really good conversation. Surprise means there's something about the question that is attention-grabbing. Specific means that we narrow the question from a broad focus to a very narrow focus. Personal means that the question includes something that requires a personal response, not a theoretical response.

For example:

FROM...	TO...
Don't you just hate people who judge other people?	When have you experienced judgment as both a good thing and a bad thing in your life?
How was your day?	What's something that happened today that made you want to pray?
What was your childhood like?	If you had to choose one experience in your childhood that shaped who you've become more than any other experience, what would it be?
How many pets do you have?	What's one way your pets have changed your life for the better, and one way they've made it harder?

You'll notice my last two examples have nothing overtly to do with Jesus—we ask pursuit questions to both explore Jesus more deeply with others and to lay the groundwork for that kind of conversation. The goal is to dig past the surface soil and get to the rich stuff underneath. Good questions stimulate courage in those who respond to them.

My rule of thumb in any conversation is simple: *Always ask one more follow-up question than you normally would.*

• We subversively guide the discussion by asking great follow-up questions. My rule of thumb in any conversation is simple: *Always ask one more follow-up question than you normally would.* When we pursue past our normal boundaries, we unlock treasure. And when an answer seems out of place or incongruous, we can redirect the flow of the conversation by asking a follow-up question like: "If _____ is true, then how can _____ also be true?" The key is to pay attention well, and then always ask follow-up questions until you hit a brick wall. Most of us give up way too soon. People are always dropping clues about what's really going on in their lives when we're in conversation with them. We simply don't target those clues often enough by asking follow-up questions. Common pursuit-clues people throw out include: "That's another story…" and "But we don't need to talk about that…" and "Fine" or "I've been better…" (in answer to "How are you?") and "That's a long story…" and "You don't want to know…" These are all vulnerability strategies that function like camouflaged invitations—we are too insecure to invite deep engagement, so we drop clues as invitations to others to pursue us within a context of emotional safety.

"I have added a simple element to my time with Jesus—I take five minutes to just be quiet and listen. Because my mind wanders so much, a couple of minutes into that time I begin an entry in my journal: 'Son…' and ask Jesus to speak to me. With that, I just begin to write what comes to mind. The result has been a much closer connection to Jesus, as well as more fruit produced by my actions." —Scott Larson

On my way to a conference in a remote Canadian city, I rode in a van for an hour next to a 17-year-old student named Trevor. I spent about 40 minutes of that hour asking Trevor "next questions." When I asked him why he was traveling so far to attend the conference, he told me he used to go to the Christian high school that's attached to the college and was looking forward to seeing his friends again. He left school before finishing his final year because he had an incredible job opportunity in the oil industry. No, he had no regrets about leaving early because he was making really good money.

We are too insecure to invite deep engagement, so we drop clues as invitations to others to pursue us within a context of emotional safety.

Something about his story left an aftertaste of dissonance in me, so I pursued possible alternatives to the reason he gave me for leaving school. He told me he didn't get along well with his parents. When I asked why, he thought for a while and then said, "They just have different morals than me." So I asked, "Are your morals better or worse than theirs?" He then described his parents as ultraconservative Christians who were unrealistic and inflexible. And our conversation went deep from there. Because I repeatedly asked the next question with Trevor, he let me see some of his treasure.

• **We ignore false humility and pride and then tell our own mid-stream story.** It's tempting to gravitate to extremes in conversations—either we hang back because of false humility, or we dominate because of pride. We're called to live in the holy middle between these extremes, where we'll share our own raw story if we expect others to share their story. It's not true humility to only pursue others and never allow ourselves to be pursued. And it's not true humility to hijack a conversation by making it about us: "I know exactly what you mean—the same thing happened to me..."

• **Courage demands that we respond to oversimplified or poorly reasoned responses by asking people to take another shot at it.** C.S. Lewis' razor intellect was molded by the tutor he lived with for years—the man nicknamed "The Great Knock" (William T. Kirkpatrick). Nervous about meeting the man, Lewis attempted some awkward conversation after he got off the train and introduced himself to Kirkpatrick: "I said I was surprised at the 'scenery' of Surrey; it was much 'wilder' than I had expected. 'Stop!' shouted Kirk with a suddenness that made me jump. 'What do you mean by wildness and what ground had you for not expecting it?' "[1] The Great Knock had no patience for fuzzy answers or lazy observations. It's obviously risky to respond to people the way the Great Knock would, but we can certainly encourage them, gently, to think past their pat answers to our questions and think more deeply.

"For 40 years, I've continued to meet with five men who live in the Northwest U.S. They have been a source of modeling, encouragement, strength, laughter, purpose, sharing sorrows and joys, and pulling one another out of ditches. They inspire me, and remind me of Jesus."
—Bob Krulish

• **We celebrate fearless insights when we hear them.** Nothing fuels fearless conversations more than celebrating the fearless things people say. Simply telling someone the truth—"Wow, I really appreciate your honesty about that"—can have a profound impact on the depth of our conversations.

The more we maintain our stamina in our conversations with people, asking observant and Jesus-esque questions and looking for little portals into their soul, the more we feel the deep joy that a fearless, garage-band way of engaging others brings.

Endnotes

1 C.S. Lewis, *Surprised by Joy* (Orlando, FL: Harcourt, 1955), 133.

—23—

Ignoring Funhouse Mirrors

"Our stories are being hijacked. We need to take them back."

—Gary Friesen

We're surrounded by mirrors—though, unless you're a supermodel or a solar-panel installer, I mean that symbolically. We all have mirrors surrounding us that are trying to tell us who we are, and almost all of those mirrors give a false reflection of our true beauty. We won't discover the truth about who we are, or the truth about others, by focusing on the number of Facebook friends we have, or how fast our career is advancing, or how soon a friend texts us back, or how well we attract the attention of the opposite sex, or how quickly we can run a mile, or how beautiful our home renovations turned out, or whether we have an app on our phone that our friends have never heard of, and on and on. All of the mirrors that promise to define us, except for one, are funhouse mirrors—they're warped, and therefore reflect a false and distorted image of who we really are.

> ## All of the mirrors that promise to define us, except for one, are funhouse mirrors— they're warped, and therefore reflect a false and distorted image of who we really are.

The one exception is Jesus. He alone is the only trustworthy mirror for who we really are. When he declared that he had come to set captives free (Luke 4:18), one of his targets was certainly the captivity we experience by living inside a false identity—a distorted image of who we are. This is evident when Jesus infuriates the Pharisees by offering forgiveness, not healing, to a paralytic man whose friends have brought him to the Master for a miraculous physical restoration. Jesus responds with this: "Which is easier: to say, 'Your sins are forgiven,' or to say, 'Get up and walk' "? (Matthew 9:5, NIV). Our core need, just as important as physical healing, is forgiveness that leads to a restored relationship with Jesus, who then restores our true identity as God's beloved. We're as equally paralyzed by the damage to our identity as we are damaged by physical paralysis. Jesus wants to answer our deepest questions: "Who am I?" and "Am I treasured?" And he wants us to taste and see him well enough that we begin to trust the mirror he holds up to our identity.

"Marriage is a profound mirror in my life—I see my failures and fragility, and Alyssa constantly encourages me and pushes me more toward Jesus." —Jefferson Bethke

When Nicodemus the Pharisee visits Jesus under the cloak of darkness to ask him questions about who he is and what he intends to do, Jesus condenses all realities into one simple reality: "You must be born again." Here he's pulling back the curtain on what's really going on in our lives, and in the spiritual world that encloses our physical world: We're caught up in a war that is waged on the battlefield of our identity. There is a one true God who loves us and is bent on restoring us into relationship with him by redeeming our broken identity. The essence of who we are must be born again. And we have a killing, stealing, and destroying enemy who is intent on distorting our identity (and the identity of Jesus) so completely that we forget we were made for God's pleasure.

The essence of who we are must be born again.

This explains why so many of us struggle to understand and embrace our true identity as beloved children of God. In the enemy territory that is our life on earth, we're caught in a swirl of voices, all demanding the right to *identify* us.

- The advertisers that invade every nook and cranny of our lives (we're exposed to more than 12,000 direct and indirect marketing messages every day) would like us to believe that consumption is central to our identity.

- The voices of authority in our lives would like us to believe that our performance is the only true mark of our identity.

- Our families often insist that our true identity is whatever they decided it was when we were children.

- The music we listen to, either directly or indirectly, encourages us to believe that our sexuality and our ability to exert power over others is indicative of our true value.

- TV shows and films we watch often force us into a passive comparison with people who are richer, more attractive, more interesting, more risky, and more successful than we are.

- Our enemies in life would like us to believe that we're no more valuable than a piece of garbage or a landscaping problem that needs to be bulldozed.

- Social media mirrors back to us that, in comparison, other people have much richer and broader friendships—and are doing much more interesting things with their lives—than we are.

God's enemy practices a strategic leverage in our lives; if he can poison our true identity, we'll push the self-destruct button ourselves.

And, of course, these are just the obvious voices. There's no space to catalog all the hundreds of more subtle identity-shaping influences we experience every day. And God's enemy practices a strategic leverage in our lives; if he can poison our true identity, we'll push the self-destruct button ourselves. When we believe what isn't true about ourselves, or undergird what is not true about others, we sabotage the redemptive work of God in us and in them. But when we pursue an answer to the question "Who does Jesus say I am?" and then help others do the same, we are saving lives—our own and others. We need to hear the voice of Jesus naming us, just as he did with Peter, because his reflection of our identity will shatter the false beliefs we've embraced about ourselves, including:

- "You'll never be good enough."
- "Your performance is what's important, not your effort."
- "You damage and spoil everything you touch."
- "The reason you're treated badly by others is because they see who you really are."
- "People will always let you down, so you'd better protect yourself with self-reliance."
- "The reflection you see in the mirror is so flawed that you may never find someone to love you."

One aspect of our calling, and of our true identity that is hidden in Jesus, is to mirror back to others something closer to the beautiful truth about themselves. We do this when we yield to the Spirit of Jesus within us as we experience people and then speak out the truth about who they are. This is one area where it's not enough to let our actions do the talking—in his letter to the Roman believers, Paul said: "Faith comes from hearing" (Romans 10:17). We all need faith to believe the truth about ourselves, and the strength of our faith is tied to what we hear. So, simply, we're living as the body of Christ when we proactively "taste" goodness in others and then describe that taste to them so they can hear it. The rhythm is simple, but it will require a decision to get used to it in the beginning.

Whenever we're experiencing someone (a clerk at a store or a friend or a neighbor or a co-worker or a person we just met on the bus), we simply ask ourselves: "What word expresses what I am experiencing in this person—something I appreciate or enjoy?" Then simply reflect back that word, conversationally, to the person. For example, here are a few things I've "mirrored" to people in the last week:

I love how curious you are.

You know, a lot of people hear things that are challenging, but you almost always do something as a result of what you hear.

There's no problem in the world that wouldn't benefit from a little more of you.

The people around you sense that you can be counted on.

You've taught me so much about creativity.

Ⓙ

"I surround myself with mature believers who are like-minded and prepared to teach, encourage, and challenge me. I am one of those people who sense the presence of Jesus more when I am with other believers who can represent his Body to me than when I am in solitude. Since God made us physical beings, I don't think his goal for our spiritual growth is to learn how to relate to our invisible spiritual friend Jesus apart from his visible physical presence through his Body and Bride."   —Bruxy Cavey

If you had been a teenager when I was a teenager, I would have thought I'd won the lottery if you were my friend.

No one has had a more profound influence on my life, besides my wife, than you.

You have a gift for writing in a deeply authentic way—you penetrate to the marrow when you write.

I saw how patient you were with that person. I just want you to know I noticed, and I really admire how you carried yourself.

I never, ever consider whether or not you're giving your best effort—I always know you will.

This practice simply involves two easy-to-adopt relational habits:

1. Notice what we notice about people.

2. Find a way to express what we notice.

We're studying people and then listening for the voice of Jesus to offer a more trustworthy reflection of them.

When we do this, we will slowly, methodically draw others' attention away from funhouse mirrors, encouraging them to accept their reflection mirrored in the person of Jesus, who lives within us. This way of engaging others may seem like mere affirmation, but it goes much deeper than that. We're studying people and then listening for the voice of Jesus to offer a more trustworthy reflection of them. Over time, this diminishes the power of warped reflections in their lives, and de-captives them.

—24—

Playing Sherlock

"How often have I said to you that when you have eliminated the impossible, whatever remains, however improbable, must be the truth?"

—Sherlock Holmes

Sherlock Holmes is a lot like Batman. Yes, they each wear an iconic costume, but that's trivial. Here's their crucial same-ness: Lacking a superpower, they each practice an eccentric commitment to a skill that, in their own disparate ways, sets captives free. In the case of Mr. Holmes, it's a hyper-focused and detailed attention to others' behavior, personality, and psychology. It's his eccentric commitment to noticing the details about people that others miss that sets Holmes apart and elevates his impact in the world. The source of his renown is his incredible attention to detail—he notices more than anybody else, so he can infer the truth about things better than anybody else. It's a fictional example of a universal truth: We unlock people when we pay better attention to them than anyone else does.

Elevated impact is the natural outcome of a way-beyond-normal passion for Jesus that, in turn, fuels a way-beyond-normal love for his sheep. And those who practice a Sherlock-like commitment to seeing people well help unlock the truth about their God-given identity, freeing them from the prison of their false identity. The restoration of true identity—our own and others'—is the epic adventure we're invited into as we sink deeper into the Jesus-centered life. But if we're going to help de-captive others, we'll need new ways to channel our eccentric commitment to unlocking them. And we do this not merely because it's a more engaged way to relate to people;

we do it because "Who does Jesus say that I am?" is a pursuit that captures the heart of Jesus-centered people.

If we're going to capture and communicate what is beautiful and true about others—the seeds Jesus has planted in them—we'll need to pay way, way better attention to the details of their often-subtle distinctives.

This way of relating with people is mapped out by science writer Maria Konnikova's book *Mastermind: How to Think Like Sherlock Holmes*. In it, she extracts the embedded habits of eccentric-pursuit people...

1. **Be obsessively observant.** Konnikova writes:

It's not just about the passive process of letting people enter into your visual field. It is about knowing what and how to observe and directing your attention accordingly: What details do you focus on? What details do you omit? And how do you take in and capture those details that you do choose to zoom in on?[1]

If we're going to capture and communicate what is beautiful and true about others—the seeds Jesus has planted in them—we'll need to pay way, way better attention to the details of their often-subtle distinctives. What makes them unique? What strengths do they have to give? What is delightful about them, even if it's buried under defense mechanisms? The more we pay close attention to the people we relate to, the more the details of their idiosyncrasies, their passions, their assumptions about life, and their wounds rise to the surface, where we can explore them. This is exactly how Jesus related to the people around him, time after time—his encounter with the woman at the well is a quintessential example, but you can see this pattern in every interchange.

2. **Be selective.** Konnikova writes:

Our brains are bombarded by something like 11 million pieces of data—that is, items in our surroundings that come at all of our senses—at once. Of that, we are able to consciously process only about 40. What that basically means is that we "see" precious little of what's around us, and what we think of as objective seeing would better be termed selective filtering—and our state of mind, our mood, our thoughts at any given moment, our motivation, and our goals can make it even more picky than it normally is.[2]

So it's crucial to decide to pay better attention to others, because we're prone to selectively filter them. A simple strategy: Do whatever it takes to maintain focus on the person in front of you (eyes on eyes, and no device-distractions), and ask lots of questions. Think of question-asking as if it were an Olympic sport and you're competing for the gold medal. The more questions you ask, the more you learn what's "under the hood" with each person.

3. **Be objective.** Konnikova writes:

Setting your goals beforehand will help you direct your precious attentional resources properly. It should not be an excuse to reinterpret objective facts to mesh with what you want or expect to see. Observation and deduction are two separate, distinct steps—in fact, they don't even come one right after the other.[3]

Bottom line: Approach your eccentric commitment to observing and mirroring truth to others with an open, curious, and unresolved attitude. Lay down your preconceptions, no matter how confident you are of them, and take in new information.

4. **Stay engaged.** Konnikova writes:

When we are engaged in what we are doing, all sorts of things happen. We persist longer at difficult problems—and become more likely to solve them. We experience something that psychologist Tory Higgins refers to as "flow," a presence of mind that not only allows us to extract more from whatever it is we are doing but also makes us feel better and happier: we derive actual, measurable hedonic value from the strength of our active involvement in and attention to an activity, even if the activity is as boring as sorting through stacks of mail.[4]

Persistent engagement—what Edwin Friedman calls stamina—leads to an enjoyable flow in our conversations. As I write these words, I'm sitting on an airplane next to a woman named MaryAnn; we just met 45 minutes ago. She's traveling from Denver to Michigan to visit family, whom she hasn't seen in two years. She manages a grocery store deli in a mountain town four hours from the airport. She has a master's degree and a teaching certificate, but she's bounced around a wide diversity of jobs. Her husband is staying home to care for their pets while she's away for 10 days. She asks if I'm traveling for business—I tell her I'm going to Detroit to lead a gathering of ministry leaders through an eight-hour learning experience. She asks what "religion" I am, and I tell her "Christian." She then tells me she was raised Pentecostal but doesn't go to church anymore. And now I have more than enough interesting clues to persistently pursue her story.

I learn about her spiritual journey—still full of questions and confusion and experimentation. I learn about her difficult childhood, enduring the divorce of her parents and the "selfishness" of her mother, from whom she is still estranged. At the end, I loop back to her question about my "religion" and tell her that's actually an awkward word for me, because what I really care about is pursuing a deeper relationship with Jesus, not the tips-and-techniques of a religion. Her eyes brighten and her soul sort of *exhales* when I say this. She wants to learn more and is curious about the books I've written, so I give her a card with my website and other contact information. She is thinking about Jesus for the first time in years, and she is awake and alive the way we are when we experience flow in a conversation.

"I listen. I make a habit of listening to words that drop into my mind, threads of songs that return to me, or words spoken by another that ring true. I lean in and listen deeper. I pay attention to my tears, surges of energy, knots in my stomach, or other bodily sensations. I trust that as someone created to be body and mind and soul, Jesus interacts with me in a physical sort of way sometimes. So I listen to my body as a venue for more conversation with him." —Kelley Nikondeha

Persistent pursuit will set us apart from every other person in another's life. You see this same force at work in Jesus, who persistently pursued (way more than those around him) the Samaritan woman of Sychar, Nicodemus, Peter, the Canaanite woman who asked him to eject a demon from her daughter, Zacchaeus, and on and on.

Persistent pursuit will set us apart from every other person in another's life.

Do we give up our commitment to passionate observation when our early returns are dismal, or do we persist? Back to Jesus' encounter with the woman at the well... He did not use X-ray vision to see inside the woman's soul; he simply paid ridiculous attention to her: "Come and see a man who told me everything I ever did!" (John 4:29, NLT). Those who persist best make the biggest impact, because their persistence gives others a chance to experience, and be transformed by, Jesus.

> "I seek community. Jesus always speaks to me through fellow brothers and sisters in Christ." —Jefferson Bethke

The end game for the Trinity is a restored intimacy—the kind of "me in you, you in me" relationship that we were created to enjoy in the first place. The path toward this restoration is the ridiculous-attention pursuit of Jesus, and of others. Intimacy with Jesus frees us to find restored intimacy with others.

Endnotes

1 Maria Konnikova, *Mastermind: How to Think Like Sherlock Holmes* (New York, NY: Penguin Books, 2013), 64.

2 Ibid, 77.

3 Ibid, 84.

4 Ibid, 98.

25

Offering Your Inexplicable Belief

"Finding Nemo gives us our mission in life. We want to help people get home."

—Bob Goff

Ever had someone believe in you more than you believe in yourself?

Or, even deeper, ever had someone invest *inexplicable* belief in who you are and what you can do?

I've written many books over the years, but *Sifted* was my first attempt to write something for a wider readership than the ministry community. That means every aspect of my journey, from empty page to finished manuscript, felt dangerously vulnerable. I'd never felt more simultaneously alive and afraid in my life. So you can imagine what it was like to submit that manuscript to the publisher and then wait for my editor's initial feedback. In that liminal space, my over-invested response expectation was measured first in minutes, then in hours, then in days, and then (almost intolerably) in weeks. And when the weeks rolled up into a full month of tortured waiting, "the silence" (as writer George Barzan first declared) "was deafening."

I'd never felt more simultaneously alive and afraid in my life.

Silence in our feedback loop makes the soil of our souls rich for growing the destructive narratives that haunt our lives. Destructive narratives are the obvious and diabolical lies that nevertheless seem powerfully plausible to us, and they require very little pretext before they gain traction in us. In the vacuum of that season of my life, the destructive narratives that insinuated themselves into my soul included these plausibilities...

• Maybe I'm hearing nothing because the book is *that* bad—he's embarrassed to have to tell me the bad news.

• Maybe I'm hearing nothing because the book is so full of holes that it's taking him forever to mark all the corrections and questions.

• Maybe I'm hearing nothing because I never should've attempted something so clearly beyond my abilities.

• Maybe I'm hearing nothing because the deepest things I have to give are...an embarrassment.

When the response finally came from John Blase, my editor, it was ridiculously brief, given the weight I'd loaded into the waiting. It showed up in my inbox on December 8, 2010—I know this because I've kept it in my "save forever" file.

"I should have your manuscript back to you by next Friday—I just finished another read and, man, it's the cleanest manuscript I've ever edited here (so there will be precious few edits) and it contains the strongest message of all the books I've ever worked on... I'll be proud to see it come to pass (no, I'm not blowing up your skirt)."

It's hard to accept our impossible reality when someone we trust expresses *inexplicable belief* in who we are.

After I cleared my tears, I read and reread that note—just like B. Raymond Buxton, the California man who sat in front of his computer for hours checking and rechecking the numbers after he discovered they matched one of the largest Powerball prizes in history. To a soul braced to hear the worst, John's words were like a found fortune. And just like the surreal feeling Mr. Buxton must have had, sitting there wide-eyed and gape-mouthed in front of his computer, it's hard to accept our impossible reality when someone we trust expresses *inexplicable belief* in who we are. I don't mean inexplicable in the sense that it's a belief tied to something ridiculous or nonexistent—rather, I mean a kind of belief that is so transforming that it makes mere affirmation seem shallow. It's belief that goes beyond our own assessments of our ability and impact and character, and is therefore hard for us to accept or embrace. It's a too-good-to-be-true game-changer.

"A friend told me that one secret for keeping her marriage fresh is that she takes long walks to get away from her husband. My wife didn't say this, honest... I would turn that around. I take long walks so that I can talk out loud with Jesus, and they draw me closer to him. At first people cast me some strange looks, so I take my dog along now. They assume I'm talking to him. The more I get to know Jesus, the more I want to tell him what he means to me, what I'm battling, and then listen for his voice." —Phil Callaway

When we have pursued people closely enough to uncover the treasures of their heart, we have a platform to give them the gift of inexplicable belief. At writer Donald Miller's Storyline Conference, *Love Does* author Bob Goff shared the secret sauce in his approach to a life bent on setting captives free: "What if, when people meet us, they feel like they have just met heaven? I mean, we tell people who they are turning into. We see people as who they can be. We recognize that they don't want to be told what they want—instead, we tell them who they are...and who they are turning into."[1] Paying peculiar attention to people gives them a taste of heaven. Most people, on most days, don't have anyone paying close attention to what they say or who they are or what's most enjoyable about them. When we do pay close attention, they bloom like flowers under a spring rain. And since beauty is always in the details, we'll have to notice the details of others to draw out their beauty.

Marcus Buckingham and Donald O. Clifton, authors of the bestselling business book *Now Discover Your Strengths,* popularized a profound truth that meshes well with Goff's vision for missional engagement with people.

It's a truth that Jesus buried in a strange little story called the Parable of the Weeds, recorded in Matthew 13:24-30 (NIV).

"The kingdom of heaven is like a man who sowed good seed in his field. But while everyone was sleeping, his enemy came and sowed weeds among the wheat, and went away. When the wheat sprouted and formed heads, then the weeds also appeared.

"The owner's servants came to him and said, 'Sir, didn't you sow good seed in your field? Where then did the weeds come from?'

" 'An enemy did this,' he replied.

"The servants asked him, 'Do you want us to go and pull them up?'

" 'No,' he answered, 'because while you are pulling the weeds, you may uproot the wheat with them. Let both grow together until the harvest. At that time I will tell the harvesters: First collect the weeds and tie them in bundles to be burned; then gather the wheat and bring it into my barn.' "

"I get together with others who love and follow Jesus for moments when we 'experience together' his presence—we 'listen together' to receive his guidance." —Jonathan Salgado

One way to interpret this parable is to see it through the filter of strengths and weaknesses. What if Jesus is essentially saying: "Don't pay attention to the bad stuff—the weeds; instead, concentrate on nurturing the good stuff. I'll take care of the bad stuff later on." Buckingham and Clifton make the case that the best way to profoundly influence people is to discover their strengths and fuel them, not look for their weaknesses and try to remove or improve them. Organizations that shift their attention from trying to attack their workers' weaknesses and instead concentrate on fueling their strengths experience remarkable success.[2] Translated for everyday life, this mindset means we look for evidence of the kingdom of God in the people who live in our circle of relationships and then speak it out to them, habitually and regularly. We recognize their "weeds," but we concentrate on growing their "wheat" instead (just as the Stockdale Paradox guides us to recognize brutal realities while simultaneously offering prevailing hope). Put another way, we help them discover who they are rather than harp on who they aren't.

We look for evidence of the kingdom of God in the people who live in our circle of relationships and then speak it out to them, habitually and regularly.

In practice, this means we trust the Spirit of Jesus within us to recognize and celebrate his character qualities when they surface in others. Here's a sampler of what this might look like...

• **When we're relating with people, we use stronger language than we normally would to describe what we notice.** Frankly, this is a natural strength of my Irish-Italian wife. When our two girls want to share an important accomplishment with someone, they gravitate to Bev more than to me. That's because she fully enters into that moment with them—metaphorically, she expands the boundaries of what is beautiful about them, so they get a clearer reflection of themselves. Yesterday my 12-year-old daughter, Emma, came home from school and immediately wanted to tell someone about the 100 she got on her last math test. Of course, she sought out Bev first, who reacted with typical abandon: "Emma! That's incredible—you have worked SO hard to get better in math. You have shown so much perseverance and determination. Way to go, girl!" I watched as Emma's spirit inflated like a balloon. Bev didn't merely applaud her performance; she recognized the character qualities of Jesus in her and used strong language to celebrate what she saw.

• **Ask Jesus to give us a word of inexplicable belief for the people who move in and out of our lives, and then make a point to share that word face-to-face or write it in a text or email or handwritten card.** This may mean we use our "gap moments" in everyday life to mull over our interactions with others, asking the Spirit to describe for us their wheat. Then we simply follow up by taking 30 seconds to communicate what we discover about them. The other day I recommended a friend at work for a creative new project. I later told him exactly how I described him to the person who was inquiring about him: "You're going after the right person—he's not only one of the most creative, out-of-the-box people I've ever met, he knows how to get things done." My intention was to *mark* my friend's God-given gifts and express my deep and unwavering belief in him.

• **Stand up at celebrations (birthday, wedding, anniversary, funeral, Mother's Day, or Father's Day, for example) and offer a more formal statement of inexplicable belief on behalf of the honored person.** I once attended a funeral of someone I didn't know all that well. When the officiating pastor asked the gathered friends and family to offer words of reflection and appreciation for this woman, no one in the room, including members of her extended family, stood to offer anything. In the midst of a long and awkward silence, I couldn't simply let the moment pass—I thought about my brief "tastes" of this woman's essential beauty and rose from my seat at the back of the sanctuary to speak out what I enjoyed about her. Later, her family members told me they felt too much sadness to say anything when they had the chance. Grief is overwhelming. But big moments cry out for someone to step into the gap and formally mark how the person has reflected their fearfully and wonderfully made reality. These big moments are not, of course, confined to seasons of grieving. Birthdays, anniversaries, dedications, baptisms, graduations, award ceremonies, milestones, and special events all offer opportunities to express inexplicable belief in others.

• **Pay attention to group moments, when the target of your inexplicable belief is around others, and say something specific about how that person reflects the Spirit of Jesus.** These are "cloud of witnesses" moments, and even a small observation is magnified because of the setting and context. If you have ever experienced such moments yourself, you know they are unforgettable and even transforming. My daughter Emma is a middle schooler, and her parent-teacher conferences are purposely structured to include the student as well. So we go to the school's gym where all of the teachers are sitting at stations around a huge horseshoe configuration of narrow tables. The strategy is called Arena Conferences. My wife and I wait with Emma to meet with each teacher. Some of them understand how packed with transformative power these short interactions are, and they take full advantage of their opportunity. When Emma heard two successive teachers tell her parents, while she sat next to us, that she is one of the most delightful, hard-working, funny, and engaging students they've ever had, we could see healing and transformation happen right before our eyes. Look for your own cloud-of-witnesses opportunities, and take full advantage of them when the Spirit nudges you.

We are not merely helping people move toward reconciliation with the Father through the invitation of the Son, but we are helping people reconcile themselves to their true, created beauty.

What we do in the playground of inexplicable belief flows from a foundation of remembering—we re-embrace the ministry of reconciliation we've been given by Jesus. In other words, we recognize that we are not merely helping people move toward reconciliation with the Father through the invitation of the Son, but we are helping people reconcile themselves to their true, created beauty. There is a beauty in others that is marred by sin—in some cases it has been horribly disfigured by sin. Our gift of inexplicable belief in their lives is an extension of the miraculous healing touch of Jesus—dead things come to life when he touches them. And we are conduits for his up-from-the-grave love in others' lives.

Endnotes

1 From notes on Bob Goff's lecture, taken by Tamara Park at Donald Miller's 2014 Storyline Conference.

2 Taken from *Now Discover Your Strengths* by Marcus Buckingham and Donald Clifton (New York, NY: Free Press, 2001).

26

Living Out of Your True Name

"I've talked to nearly 30,000 people on this show, and all 30,000 had one thing in common: They all wanted validation... I would tell you that every single person you will ever meet shares that common desire."

—Oprah Winfrey

If you were born a Native American 200 years ago, or a Jew 2,000 years ago, the name you received from your parents wouldn't merely express something that sounded nice, or tied to your family's history. Your name would've represented an *identity* your parents hoped you would live into. It would be less of a label and more of a prophetic description. That's because Jews and Native Americans understood something that's naturally true in the kingdom of God: *The names we embrace in life are the names we become.*

When Jesus recalibrates Simon by calling him Petros, he's not merely pulling the name out of thin air and handing it to his friend—he's *uncovering* his prophetic identity. In renaming his closest friend with a descriptive word that had never before been used as a name, Jesus answers two big questions for him: *Who am I?* and *What am I doing here?* As we name Jesus, he names us. And the name he gives us projects onto us an identity born out of his faith in us and his understanding of how our heart is wired. In the church we often talk about our faith in Jesus, but we rarely explore the biblical reality that Jesus has faith in *us*. He created in us an identity that's tied to a purpose in his kingdom, and our journey with him through life is a continuous revelation of that identity. He is bent on revealing our true name.

What if we all have two names—the one our parents gave us and the one God calls us when he's plotting his next adventure? Author and pastor Walter Wangerin says there are, universally, two creation languages. The first is spoken by God, who spoke everything into being out of nothing at all. The second is the language God first gave to Adam, the language of naming (Genesis 2). Names, says Wangerin, are not merely labels: "The thing named is brought into place so it can be known. A name establishes a person's relationship with other named things. The naming action begins to declare the person's purpose. And this naming is powerful...."[1]

We're caught in the middle of a war over our identity; in fact, every assault from hell on our lives always has a component designed to destroy our God-given identity.

If the names we embrace are the names we become, our names are the chosen battleground for God's enemy in our lives. We're caught in the middle of a war over our identity; in fact, every assault from hell on our lives always has a component designed to destroy our God-given identity. If God's enemy can pollute or destroy what is most true about us, then we'll live out of a false identity and fuel his purposes—and his purposes are to steal, kill, and destroy. This helps explain why genealogy is the second-most popular hobby in the U.S., after gardening, and the second-most visited category of websites, after pornography. It's a billion-dollar industry, even catalyzing a cottage industry in DNA ancestry testing. We have a deep hunger to reattach ourselves to the roots of our identity, to find the kind of solid footing we need to live in greater freedom and with more purpose.

This is why it's so crucial for us to not only discover, embrace, and live out of our own true name (our embedded identity in Jesus), but to help others do the same.

Jesus wants to reveal to us who we are and what we're made to do. And because the Spirit of Jesus who lives within us is radically generous, we're compelled by generosity to help in his unveiling of others in our lives. J.R.R. Tolkien's powerful conclusion to the *Lord of the Rings* fantasy saga is really the story of a man breaking free of the false identity of a name that diminishes him (Aragorn, who has embraced the name "Strider" instead of his true name, and spends his life roaming the wilderness as a "ranger"). Unless Aragorn steps into his true identity as the king, leading the forces of good against the forces of evil (embodied by a Satan-like entity named Sauron), all that he loves will be lost. But Aragorn is afraid to become what he was meant to be, because the mirror of Strider tells him his cowardly ancestors define who he is. But then a wise, older mentor calls him out.

"For a time I awoke each morning miserable, mulling over what I had to accomplish and who I had to impress that day. Increasingly, I'm learning how to wake up each morning and direct my first thoughts to Christ. I thank him for all he's done and is doing for me. There is a measurable difference in the next 24 hours." —Phil Callaway

In one of the film's climactic scenes, Aragorn is summoned to a battlefield tent where he finds a hooded figure, the elven Lord Elrond, waiting for him. He's there to challenge Aragorn to embrace his true identity, because the fate of the world hangs on his leadership. Elrond hands Aragorn a sword called Anduril, a legendary weapon wielded by the great kings of Gondor:

Aragorn: *(Takes the sword, staring at it in wonder.)* Sauron will not have forgotten the sword of Elendil. *(He draws the long blade from its sheath.)* The blade that was broken shall return to Minas Tirith.

Elrond: The man who can wield the power of this sword can summon to him an army more deadly than any that walks this earth. *(Elrond stares hard at Aragorn.)* Put aside the Ranger—become who you were born to be... *(A heavy silence hangs in the room.)*[2]

Of course, Aragorn goes on to assume the mantle of king and lead the forces of good to victory over Sauron and the forces of darkness. When I show this powerful scene to groups, I ask them to focus on how Elrond forces a turning point in Aragorn's life. He challenges Aragorn to step fully into his true identity—his true name. And here Tolkien is embedding a theological and biblical reality inside his epic story of sin and redemption.

When you consider "Who does Jesus say that I am?" do you have a sense of what is most deeply true about your identity?

Has God ever answered this overshadowing question in your life? When you consider "Who does Jesus say that I am?" do you have a sense of what is most deeply true about your identity?

I remember my own "Aragorn moment" well. It was early in my marriage. I was speaking at a youth ministry conference—the last place I wanted to be at that moment in my life. My wife and I were in the throes of a significant challenge to our young marriage. Our arguments were getting more and more damaging. Just before my ride to the airport showed up, we were locked in the most destructive conflict we'd ever had. I had a sinking feeling that we'd crossed a line in our relationship, and then the doorbell rang. I left for the speaking trip upset and worried; I could sense our relationship was in danger, and it was killing me. I mean, I literally felt like someone was jamming a dagger into my gut. When I landed, I called my wife to reconnect—she hung up on me. I called back, and she hung up again. I could not fix our problems long-distance, so I was sentenced to three days of agony. I walked through the halls of the convention center hoping no one would recognize me so I wouldn't have to talk with anyone. My interior conversation was full of self-accusations and criticism. My identity was under full-scale assault, and shame was quickly sinking me.

It was during one of my wall-hugging walks down a crowded hallway that I felt Jesus nudging me to go into an empty conference room and close the door. I sat cross-legged on the floor in semi-darkness, with the legal pad and pen I'd been carrying. And then Jesus spoke to me like a lightning bolt—it was one of those moments in life when I could recognize his voice as if it was audible. I scribbled down what I was hearing. His voice was so clear that it felt like simply taking dictation. And I couldn't have been more shocked (and named) by what I sensed. Here's what I wrote:

You're a quarterback. You see the field. You're squirming away from the rush to find space to release the ball. You never give up. You have courage in the face of ferocity—in fact, ferocity draws out your courage. You want to score even when the team is too far behind for it to matter. You love the thrill of creating a play in the huddle, under pressure, and spreading the ball around to everyone on the team. You have no greater feeling than throwing the ball hard to a spot and watching the receiver get to it without breaking stride. In fact, you love it most when the receiver is closely covered and it takes a perfect throw to get it to him. You have the same feeling when you throw a bomb and watch the receiver run under it, or when you tear away from the grasp of a defender, or when you see and feel blood on your elbows or knees and feel alive because of it. You love to score right after the other team has scored, but you want to do it methodically, first down by first down, right down the field. You love fourth down! You want to win, but you're satisfied by fighting well.

What I craved was the voice of Jesus telling me everything was going to be okay. But that's not what happened. Instead, he named me, using words that are still so personal that it's hard to read them without crying. With this description he captured my essence the same way "Petros" captured the essence of Simon—*and he saved my life.* I returned home from the conference, and my wife asked me to move out. Our problems were not magically fixed because of my intimate experience with Jesus on that conference-room floor. We spent three months separated, with the leverage of pain driving us more deeply into counseling as we tried to grapple with the wounds that were fueling our fights.

"I talk out loud and in my head and heart to him all the time, without feeling like I always have to set aside time to 'pray.' " —Kathy Escobar

What emerged in me during that season in the desert was not a new set of tips-and-techniques to make our relationship work better—instead, my true self emerged from the dark and came out to play. I moved back in to our home just after the holidays. This year marks our 25th wedding anniversary.

What emerged in me during that season in the desert was not a new set of tips-and-techniques to make our relationship work better—instead, my true self emerged from the dark and came out to play.

Many years after this crisis in my life, God has continued to use its brutal leverage in my soul to unveil my true identity and bring radical and beautiful change in my marriage. Of course, "Quarterback" is just a metaphor for something much more pertinent and treasured: the true nature of my heart and identity. Jesus was describing me as I *really* am. And as the years go by I yield, more and more, to my true identity.

The forming power of embracing our true name is unmistakable. There are two middle-aged brothers in my church whose last name, for most of their lives, was literally "Failure." For years they labored through life, burdened by the latent curse of their surname and sometimes unconsciously obeying its prophetic gravity. Later in life, after their wives had begged them for years to change their name, the men decided to research the origins of "Failure" and discovered it's an Americanized version of their original German surname, Fehler. When they formally adopted the German original as their last name, it's as if the sun rose over their landscape. That's because the names we embrace are the names we become.

Asking the Question

As we experiment with a more intentional and Jesus-dependent reflection of the beauty we taste in others, we move inside the boundaries of love—this means, of course, that damning, accusing words or descriptions are not from Jesus. Normal parents never describe the essence of their children with words that damn. Never. And neither does our Father in heaven.

Most people already know what's wrong with them; they know their own list of deficits very well. But they know very little about the person God has described as "fearfully and wonderfully made" (Psalm 139:14). So in addition to acting like Sherlock Holmes in their lives and helping reflect their true identity, we can also encourage them to explore the answer to this life-changing question: "Who does Jesus say I am?" Since it's never good to lead people to places we haven't first explored, it would be good to pursue this question ourselves.

Most people already know what's wrong with them; they know their own list of deficits very well. But they know very little about the person God has described as "fearfully and wonderfully made" (Psalm 139:14).

First, find a place to do this where you can have some quiet space—you need a sense of safety and isolation. Most likely, you won't find this kind of space at home during normal family time. You need an empty church during the week; or steal away early in the morning before your household comes alive, or late at night when everyone is in bed, or on a retreat when you have the luxury of solitary time. The key is to do this at a time when you're naturally at a lower energy level, and to make sure you have the physical and emotional space you need to feel alone.

You'll need something to write on and something to write with—you're going to ask Jesus an important question and listen for his response. Before you enter into this time, do two things: Assert the authority you have over your own soul and formally silence your own voice, and ask Jesus to silence the voice of the enemy in your life. Then, in the quiet, simply ask Jesus: "Who do you say I am?" Wait in silence, relaxed and unconcerned about producing anything during this time. Imagine yourself as a catcher's mitt, just waiting to receive whatever Jesus throws at you. It could be a word, a phrase, a picture of something in your mind, a Scripture passage, or a full-on description that comes to you like my quarterback moment came to me. Make sure you write down whatever you sense during this time. It's also quite possible you may not hear anything from Jesus during this time, and that's okay, too. This is not a test of your spiritual maturity—it's simply knocking on Jesus' door, just as he asks us to do.

After you have come to the natural end of this time, ask Jesus to bring to mind at least one person with whom you'd feel comfortable sharing what you received. Then go on a walk or have a cup of coffee and share what you've written—simply ask your friend to react to what you've shared. When you do, you invite others to enter into your story and affirm or even expand on your revealed identity. And, in turn, you can encourage your friends to try the same experiment for themselves.

What people most crave are relationships with people who are all-in with them—who are pursuers by their very nature. They're drawn to people who will enter into their world like missionaries, not people who offer relationship only inside their own comfort zone. They're longing, like we are, to discover their true identity, and to find out if Jesus cherishes and enjoys them. And we've been invited into that epic mission with them.

The names we embrace are the names we become.

Endnotes

1 Walter Wangerin, from a keynote address at Hutchmoot, an annual gathering organized by musician and author Andrew Peterson, August 2010.

2 Dialogue taken from the shooting script for *The Lord of the Rings: The Return of the King*, written by Fran Walsh, Philippa Boyens, and Peter Jackson, based on the book by J.R.R. Tolkien.

—A Closing Imperative—
Determining to Know Nothing

"Who matters most to you says the most about you."

—The slogan of a TV advertisement for MassMutual

Is it possible that a single, simple change to a core habit in your life could change everything for the better? In *The Power of Habit*, author Charles Duhigg calls this one thing the "keystone habit." He says: "Keystone habits start a process that, over time, transforms everything. The habits that matter most are the ones that, when they start to shift, dislodge and remake other patterns."[1] Because we are creatures of habit, and we gravitate to routines that provide order, a change to a keystone habit in our relationship with Jesus can change everything else in our lives.

When I was a kid, a magnifying glass seemed like it had a kind of magical ability. Of course, that's because I didn't really understand how it worked. The glass is slightly curved, forming a convex lens that bends the light rays from an object so it appears larger. When a magnifying glass is placed between an object and direct sunlight, it bends all those light rays into a single point, making that point really, really hot.

That's a nice description of the Christian life in full: following Jesus because we're consumed by him.

The Jesus-centered life is a lot like that magnifying glass. When we use Spurgeon's beeline as the curved lens for everything we do and put it between Jesus and our relationships, something flames up. We're continually lighting a fire in others, and in ourselves. And this particular fire is a consuming fire, which means we all end up consumed by and for Jesus. That's a nice description of the Christian life in full: following Jesus because we're consumed by him. Because we're undeniably, unapologetically Jesus-centered. We read Paul's declaration from 1 Corinthians 2—"For I determined to know nothing among you except Jesus Christ, and Him crucified"—with a deep resonance.

The normal Christian life can feel like an epic everyday adventure when you've been ruined by Jesus and ruined for Jesus. We discover that our greatest joy is simply his presence, and our greatest purpose is feeding his sheep.

Imagine for a moment you're standing on a beach at the Sea of Tiberias. You've just lived through the most spectacular stretch of days in all of history, as Jesus has suffered, died, been buried, and then resurrected. You don't know, really, what to do with your life now, so you ask your friends if they'd like to go fishing. For one night you go back to the life you knew before the hurricane of Jesus swept through your life. So you fish all night, catching nothing. And in the morning, one of your friends sees a man on the beach, watching. The man calls out to you, asking if you've fished the starboard side of the boat. *Who do you think we are, buddy*, you're thinking. *Of course we've fished the starboard side.* But you throw the nets over the side again, and they're suddenly full of thrashing fish. And your friend looks to the shore again, studying the man—he recognizes him as Jesus. So even though you're stripped naked for your work, you tie your tunic around your waist, leap over the side of the boat, and splash your way to the shore. You arrive dripping wet and full of expectation. You feel the warmth of the fire he's built, and you smell a good breakfast cooking over it. And you can't stop grinning because…it's Jesus. He's alive and smiling at you.

Then you see a grin just dawn on his face as he says, one more time, with gravity, "Feed my sheep."

A couple of your friends are putting the fire out now, and you can smell the smoke. You glance over at Jesus and realize he's staring right at you… right through you. He asks you to take a little walk with him. So you get up, but you keep looking at him because your soul is buzzing. You're walking next to Jesus again. He turns, looks at you again, and asks a question that bites a little: "Do you *truly* love me more than any other?" A little startled, you tell him…

What do you say?

In response, Jesus says: "Feed my lambs." Then you walk a little farther in silence. This time he doesn't turn to you; his eyes are focused way down the beach. He asks again: "Do you truly love me?" And you respond...

How do you respond?

Now Jesus stops and turns, his face uncomfortably close to yours. He won't take his eyes off you. "Take care of my sheep," he says. Then, leaning in slightly, he asks one more time, "Do you love me?" And you can't hide your hurt anymore. You tell him...

What do you say?

Jesus backs away slightly and looks at you with a mixture of tenderness and fierceness. Then you see a grin just dawn on his face as he says, one more time, with gravity, "Feed my sheep." There's a long pause now... You have time to ponder what it means to feed Jesus' sheep.

Then Jesus starts walking again. He gets a few yards ahead of you and you see him glance back; then he calls you by a name you've never heard before, but it nevertheless seems vaguely familiar. You look at him... He's smiling. You rush to catch up...

Endnotes

1 Charles Duhigg, *The Power of Habit: Why We Do What We Do in Life and Business* (New York, NY: Random House, 2014) 100.

Hi, reader! Rick here. I want to invite you to center on Jesus with these additional Jesus-centered resources.

JESUS-CENTERED BIBLE

Throughout the Old Testament, blue letters point out remarkable connections to Jesus, pulling you into the bigger story. And the New Testament includes a variety of thought-provoking questions that prompt us to reframe our understanding of Jesus (and ourselves).

Available in hardcover and a variety of leatherette color options.

OTHER JESUS-CENTERED RESOURCES

- **Journals** in a variety of colors—perfect for recording new insights about Jesus.
- **Devotionals**—a series of daily readings and activities for families, spouses, and Jesus-followers.
- **Coloring books**—tap into your creative side as you tap into Jesus.

To learn more about living a Jesus-centered life, visit JesusCenteredLife.com or your favorite Christian bookseller.